A HISTORY OF THE PENAL LAWS AGAINST THE IRISH CATHOLICS, FROM *THE TREATY OF LIMERICK TO THE UNION.*

By HENRY PARNELL, Esq. M. P.

"He felt it his duty to declare fully his sentiments on these points, be-
"cause he looked upon his Roman Catholic brethren as fellow subjects and
"fellow Christians, believers in the same God, and partners in the same
"Redemption. Speculative differences in some points of faith from him,
"were of no account, they and he had but one religion—the religion of
"Christianity. Therefore, as children of the same father, as travellers in
"the same road, and seekers of the same salvation, why not love each other
"as brothers? It was no part of Protestantism to persecute Catholics, and
"without justice to the Catholics there could be no security for the Protes-
"tant Establishment."——*Vide Speech of Dr. Law, Bishop of Elphin, on the Catholic Bill of* 1793.

"If any one should contend that this is not the time for Government to
"make concessions to Ireland, I wish him to consider, whether there is any
"time in which it is improper for either individuals or nations to do justice,
"any season improper for extinguishing animosity, any occasion more suit-
"able than the present, for putting an end to heart-burnings, and internal
"discontent."——*Vide Speech intended to be spoken by Dr. Watson, Bishop of Llandaff, November* 23, 1803.

THE LAWBOOK EXCHANGE, LTD.
Clark, New Jersey

ISBN 978-1-58477-310-8

Lawbook Exchange edition 2003, 2025

The quality of this reprint is equivalent to the quality of the original work.

THE LAWBOOK EXCHANGE, LTD.
33 Terminal Avenue
Clark, New Jersey 07066-1321

Please see our website for a selection of our other publications and fine facsimile reprints of classic works of legal history:
www.lawbookexchange.com

Library of Congress Cataloging-in-Publication Data

Parnell, Henry, Sir, 1776-1842.
A history of the penal laws against the Irish Catholics, from the Treaty of Limerick to the Union.
p. cm.
Originally published: Dublin: Printed by H. Fitzpatrick, 1808.
Includes bibliographical references.
ISBN 1-58477-310-3 (cloth: alk. paper)
1. Catholics—Legal status, laws, etc.—Ireland—History. 2. Dissenters, Religious—Legal status, laws, etc.—Ireland—History. I. Title.

KDK1260.C45 P37 2003
344.415'097 —dc21 2002044357

Printed in the United States of America on acid-free paper

A

HISTORY

OF THE

PENAL LAWS

AGAINST THE

IRISH CATHOLICS,

FROM

THE TREATY OF LIMERICK TO THE UNION.

By HENRY PARNELL, Esq. M. P.

"He felt it his duty to declare fully his sentiments on these points, be-
"cause he looked upon his Roman Catholic brethren as fellow subjects and
"fellow Christians, believers in the same God, and partners in the same
"Redemption. Speculative differences in some points of faith from him,
"were of no account, they and he had but one religion—the religion of
"Christianity. Therefore, as children of the same father, as travellers in
"the same road, and seekers of the same salvation, why not love each other
"as brothers? It was no part of Protestantism to persecute Catholics, and
"without justice to the Catholics there could be no security for the Protes-
"tant Establishment."——*Vide Speech of Dr. Law, Bishop of Elphin, on the Catholic Bill of* 1793.

"If any one should contend that this is not the time for Government to
"make concessions to Ireland, I wish him to consider, whether there is any
"time in which it is improper for either individuals or nations to do justice,
"any season improper for extinguishing animosity, any occasion more suit-
"able than the present, for putting an end to heart-burnings, and internal
"discontent."——*Vide Speech intended to be spoken by Dr. Watson, Bishop of Llandaff, November* 23, 1803.

DUBLIN:

PRINTED BY H. FITZPATRICK, 4, CAPEL-STREET.

1808.

A

HISTORY

OF THE

PENAL LAWS,

&c. &c.

WILLIAM III.

WHEN James abdicated the Throne of England, he retired to France, to ſolicit the aid of Louis XIV. to enable him to ſecure the poſſeſſion of Ireland, where he was ſtill acknowledged as the lawful Sovereign. On the 12th of March, 1689, James landed at Kinſale with about 1200 of his own ſubjects in the pay of France, and 100 French officers. He was received with open arms, and the whole country ſeemed to be devoted to him, for although the Proteſtants in the North had declared for the new Government, their ſtrength and number were inconſiderable, when compared with the forces of the Lord Deputy Tyrconnel. This Miniſter had diſarmed all the other Proteſtants in one day, and aſſem-

B bled

bled an army of 30,000 foot and 8000 cavalry.* Addreſſes were poured in upon James from all orders of the people. The eſtabliſhed clergy among the reſt congratulated him upon his arrival, a certain ſign that his chance of ſucceſs was not contemptible.

James continued to govern Ireland, without any interruption from William, till the 13th of Auguſt,† when Schomberg landed at Belfaſt with an Engliſh army of 10,000 men. To oppoſe him, James collected his forces amounting to 30,000 at Drogheda.‡ Schomberg who had arrived at Dundalk thought it prudent to advance no farther; and inſtead of reducing Ireland, after having loſt one half of his army by ſickneſs, he at the end of the campaign was under the neceſſity of entrenching himſelf againſt an enemy, which he had been taught in England to deſpiſe, and of confining his operations to the protection of the Northern Province.§

On the 14th of June in the year following, William landed with reinforcements at Carrickfergus. His military genius as well as the diſ-

tracted

* Smollet, 1. 36. † Leland, v. 3. b. 6. c. 6. ‡ Ib. § Ib.

tracted state of England, and the formidable preparations of France, inclined him to a vigorous prosecution of the war in Ireland.* He advanced towards Dublin with an army of 36,000 men. James collected his forces amounting to 33,000 at Drogheda, and by an unaccountable infatuation resisted the advice of his General Officers to act on the defensive against William; who would then have had to contend at the same time against a threatened foreign invasion of Britain, the insurrection which his own subjects were plotting, and the difficulty of maintaining his Irish army in an unfriendly climate without provisions or succours.

Though William obtained a decided victory at the Boyne, the Irish army had fought with courage and obstinacy; and, in consequence of having at one time repulsed the centre of the English army, were able to retire in good order, with the loss of only 1500 men.† The subsequent defeat of General Douglas before Athlone, and of William himself before Limerick, left James at the end of the campaign in possession of

* Leland, v. 3, b. 6. c. 6.

† Ib.

of nearly one half of Ireland, and well ſupported by an army inured to war and commanded by able and experienced Generals. William experienced ſtill greater embarraſſments on the Continent and in England. A victory had been gained by Luxemburgh, in Flanders, over Prince Waldeck and the confederate army; Tourville had defeated the united fleets of England and Holland; and great dejection and diſcontent was viſible among all his Britiſh ſubjects.

William having returned to England in the autumn of 1690, General Ginckle, with an army inferior to that of St. Ruth, who now commanded the Iriſh forces, commenced the campaign by the capture of the fort of Baltimore. Having afterwards taken Athlone, and defeated St. Ruth at the battle of Aughrim, he laid ſiege to Limerick on the 25th of Auguſt, 1691. The fortifications had been ſtrengthened ſince William was repulſed before it in the preceding year; the garriſon was healthy, well ſupplied, and in numbers equal to the aſſailants, and ſtrong ſuccours were daily expected from France*. The beſiegers, on the other hand, were too few for the undertaking, the

* Leland, v. 3. b. 6. c. 6.

the ſeaſon of the year was far advanced, and they had no expectations of receiving any reinforcements.

Week paſſed away after week without Ginckle's obtaining any advantage over the beſieged; at length he made a lodgment on the oppoſite ſide of the Shannon. But, notwithſtanding this ſucceſs, it was debated whether the ſiege ſhould be carried on, or converted into a blockade; ſuch were the difficulties foreſeen in reducing the town. It was dangerous for the beſiegers to continue in their preſent ſtation on the approach of winter, and hazardous to divide an army ſufficient only for aſſailing the town on one ſide; and yet the only effectual way of reducing it was to inveſt it on all ſides, by cutting off the garriſon from all intercourſe with the county of Clare*.

William, in the mean time, was ſo ſenſible of the neceſſity of obtaining the ſurrender of the Iriſh army, in order to ſecure his newly acquired throne, and the ſucceſs of the revolution, that he ſent inſtructions to the Lords Juſtices to iſſue a proclamation, offering to the Catholics ſtill more liberal

* Leland, v. 3. b. 6. c. 6.

liberal terms than thoſe which they afterwards accepted; and he gave Ginckle urgent directions to terminate the war on any conditions*. Fortunately, however, for William and the revolution party, but moſt unfortunately, as events have ſince proved, for the Catholics, the garriſon of Limerick beat a parley on the 29th day of the ſiege. A ceſſation of three days was granted; and, on the laſt day of it, the Iriſh Generals propoſed terms of capitulation. They required an act of indemnity for all paſt offences, with a full enjoyment of the eſtates they poſſeſſed before the preſent revolution, freedom for the Catholic worſhip, with an eſtabliſhment of one Romiſh eccleſiaſtic in each pariſh. They alſo required, that Catholics ſhould be declared fully qualified for every office, civil and military; that they ſhould be admitted into all corporations; and, that the Iriſh army ſhould be kept up and paid in the ſame manner with the King's other troops, provided they were willing to ſerve†. Ginckle refuſed to accede to their propoſal;

* Leland, v. 3. b. 6. c. 6. and Harris's Life of William, p. 372.

This was called the ſecret proclamation, becauſe, though printed, it never was publiſhed, in conſequence of the Lords Juſtices being informed of the inclination of the garriſon to treat for their ſurrender.

† Leland, ibid.

posal; but being desired to offer such terms as he could grant, he consented to conditions which were accepted by the garrison, and which are contained in the following civil and military articles.

Three days after they were signed, the French fleet arrived in Dingle Bay.

THE CIVIL AND MILITARY ARTICLES OF LIMERICK.

Exactly printed from the Letters Patents; wherein they are ratified and exemplified by their Majesties, under the Great Seal of England.

GULIELMUS & Maria, Dei gratia, Angliæ, Scotiæ, Franciæ & Hiberniæ Rex et Regina, Fidei Defensores, &c. Omnibus ad quos præcentes literæ nostræ pervenerint salutem: inspeximus irrotulament. quarund. literarum patentium de confirmatione, geren. dat. apud Westmonasterium vicesimo quarto die Februarii, ultimi præteriti in cancellar. nostr. irrotulat. ac ibidem de recordo remanen. in hæc verba. William and Mary, by the grace of God, &c. To all to whom these presents shall come, greeting. Whereas certain articles, bearing date the third day of October last-past, made and agreed on between our justices of our kingdom of Ireland, and our general of our forces there on the one part; and several officers there, commanding within the city of Limerick, in our said kingdom, on the other part. Whereby our said justices and general did undertake that we should ratify those articles, within the

the ſpace of eight months, or ſooner; and uſe their utmoſt endeavours that the ſame ſhould be ratified and confirmed in parliament. The tenor of which ſaid articles is as follows, viz.

ARTICLES AGREED UPON THE THIRD DAY OF OCTOBER, ONE THOUSAND SIX HUNDRED AND NINETY-ONE.

Between the Right Honourable Sir Charles Porter, Knight, and Thomas Coningſby, Eſq. Lords Juſtices of Ireland; and his Excellency the Baron De Ginckle, Lieutenant General, and Commander in Chief of the Engliſh Army; on the one Part:

And the Right Honourable Patrick Earl of Lucan, Piercy, Viſcount Gallmoy, Colonel Nicholas Purcel, Colonel Nicholas Cuſack, Sir Toby Butler, Colonel Garret Dillon, and Colonel John Brown; on the other Part:

In the behalf of the Iriſh Inhabitants in the City and County of Limerick, the Counties of Clare, Kerry, Cork, Sligo, and Mayo.

In conſideration of the Surrender of the City of Limerick, and other Agreements made between the ſaid Lieutenant General Ginckle, the Governor of the City of Limerick, and the Generals of the Iriſh army, bearing date with theſe Preſents, for the Surrender of the City, and Submiſſion of the ſaid Army: it is agreed, That,

I. THE Roman Catholics of this kingdom ſhall enjoy ſuch privileges in the exerciſe of their religion, as are conſiſtent with the laws of Ireland; or as they did enjoy in the reign of King Charles the Second: and their

their Majeſties, as ſoon as their affairs will permit them to ſummon a Parliament in this kingdom, will endeavour to procure the ſaid Roman Catholics ſuch farther ſecurity in that particular, *as may preſerve them from any diſturbance upon the account of their ſaid religion.*

II. All the inhabitants or reſidents of Limerick, or any other garriſon now in the poſſeſſion of the Iriſh, and all officers and ſoldiers, now in arms, under any commiſſion of King James, or thoſe authoriſed by him, to grant the ſame in the ſeveral counties of Limerick, Clare, Kerry, Cork, and Mayo, or any of them; and all the commiſſioned officers in their Majeſties quarters, that belong to the Iriſh regiments, now in being, that are treated with, and who are not priſoners of war, or have taken protection, and who ſhall return and ſubmit to their Majeſties obedience; and their and every of their heirs, ſhall hold, poſſeſs, and enjoy, all and every their eſtates of freehold and inheritance; and all the rights, titles and intereſt, privileges and immunities, which they, and every or any of them held, enjoyed, or were rightfully and lawfully intitled to in the reign of King Charles II. or at any time ſince, by the laws and ſtatutes that were in force in the ſaid reign of King Charles II. and ſhall be put in poſſeſſion, by order of the government, of ſuch of them as are in the King's hands, or the hands of his tenants, without being put to any ſuit or trouble therein; and all ſuch eſtates ſhall be freed and diſcharged from all arrears of crown-rents, quit-rents, and other public charges, incurred and become due ſince Michaelmas 1688, to the day of the date hereof: and all perſons comprehended in this article, ſhall have, hold, and enjoy all their goods and chattles, real and perſonal, to them, or any of them belonging, and remaining either in their own hands, or in the hands of any perſons whatſoever, in truſt for, or for the uſe of them, or any of them: and all, and every the ſaid perſons, of what profeſſion, trade, or calling ſoever they be, ſhall and may uſe, exerciſe, and practiſe their ſeveral and reſpective profeſſions, trades and callings, as freely as they did uſe, exerciſe, and enjoy the ſame in the reign of King Charles II. provided that nothing in this article contained be conſtrued to extend to, or reſtore any forfeiting perſon now out of the kingdom, except what are hereafter compriſed; provided alſo, that no perſon whatſoever ſhall have or enjoy the benefit of this article, that ſhall neglect or refuſe to take the oath of allegiance,* made by act of Parliament in England, in the firſt year of the reign of their preſent Majeſties, when thereunto required.

III. All merchants, or reputed merchants of the city of Limerick, or of any other garriſon now poſſeſſed by the Iriſh, or of any town or place in the counties of Clare or Kerry, who are abſent beyond the ſeas, that have not bore arms ſince their Majeſties declaration in February 1688, ſhall have the benefit of the ſecond article, in the ſame manner as if they were preſent; provided ſuch merchants, and reputed merchants, do repair into this kingdom within the ſpace of eight months from the date hereof.

IV. The following officers, viz. Colonel Simon Lutterel, Captain Rowland White, Maurice Euſtace of Yermanſtown,

* I *A. B.* do ſincerely promiſe and ſwear, that I will be faithful, and bear true Allegiance to their Majeſties King William and Queen Mary. So help me God.

Yermanſtown, Chieveas of Mayſtown, commonly called Mount-Leinſter, now belonging to the regiments in the aforeſaid garriſons and quarters of the Iriſh army, who were beyond the ſeas, and ſent thither upon affairs of their reſpective regiments, or the army in general, ſhall have the benefit and advantage of the ſecond article, provided they return hither within the ſpace of eight months from the date of theſe preſents, and ſubmit to their Majeſties Government, and take the above-mentioned oath.

V. That all and ſingular the ſaid perſons compriſed in the ſecond and third articles, ſhall have a general pardon of all attainders, outlawries, treaſons, miſpriſions of treaſon, premunires, felonies, treſpaſſes, and other crimes and miſdemeanours whatſoever, by them, or any of them, committed ſince the beginning of the reign of King James II. and if any of them are attainted by Parliament, the Lords Juſtices, and General, will uſe their beſt endeavours to get the ſame repealed by Parliament, and the outlawries to be reverſed gratis, all but writing-clerks fees.

VI. And whereas theſe preſent wars have drawn on great violences on both parts; and that if leave were given to the bringing all ſorts of private actions, the animoſities would probably continue that have been too long on foot, and the public diſturbances laſt: for the quieting and ſettling therefore of this kingdom, and avoiding thoſe inconveniencies which would be the neceſſary conſequence of the contrary, no perſon or perſons whatſoever, compriſed in the foregoing articles, ſhall be ſued, moleſted, or impleaded at the ſuit of any party or parties whatſoever, for any treſpaſſes by them committed, or for any arms, horfes, money, goods, chattles, merchandizes, or provifions whatfoever, by them feized or taken during the time of the war. And no perfon or perfons whatfoever, in the fecond or third articles comprifed, fhall be fued, impleaded, or made accountable for the rents or mean rates of any lands, tenements, or houfes, by him or them received, or enjoyed in this kingdom, fince the beginning of the prefent war, to the day of the date hereof, nor for any wafte or trefpafs by him or them committed in any fuch lands, tenements, or houfes: and it is alfo agreed, that this article fhall be mutual and reciprocal on both fides.

VII. Every nobleman and gentleman comprifed in the faid fecond and third articles, fhall have liberty to ride with a fword, and cafe of piftols, if they think fit; and keep a gun in their houfes, for the defence of the fame, or for fowling.

VIII. The inhabitants and refidents in the city of Limerick, and other garrifons, fhall be permitted to remove their goods, chattles and provifions, out of the fame, without being viewed and fearched, or paying any manner of duties, and fhall not be compelled to leave the houfes or lodgings they now have, for the fpace of fix weeks next enfuing the date hereof.

IX. The oath to be adminiftered to fuch Roman Catholics as fubmit to their Majefties Government, fhall be the oath abovefaid, and no other.

X. No perfon or perfons who fhall at any time hereafter break thefe articles, or any of them, fhall

thereby

thereby make, or cause any other person or persons to forfeit or lose the benefit of the same.

XI. The Lords Justices and General do promise to use their utmost endeavours, that all the persons comprehended in the above-mentioned articles, shall be protected and defended from all arrests and executions for debt or damage, for the space of eight months next ensuing the date hereof.

XII. Lastly, the Lords Justices and General do undertake, that their Majesties will ratify these articles within the space of eight months, or sooner, and use their utmost endeavours that the same shall be ratified and confirmed in Parliament.

XIII. And whereas Colonel John Brown stood indebted to several Protestants, by judgments of record, which appearing to the late Government, the Lord Tyrconnel, and Lord Lucan, took away the effects the said John Brown had to answer the said debts, and promised to clear the said John Brown of the said debts; which effects were taken for the public use of the Irish, and their army: for freeing the said Lord Lucan of his said engagement, past on their public account, for payment of the said Protestants, and for preventing the ruin of the said John Brown, and for satisfaction of his creditors, at the instance of the Lord Lucan, and the rest of the persons aforesaid, it is agreed, that the saids Lords Justices, and the said Baron De Ginckle, shall intercede with the King and Parliament, to have the estates secured to Roman Catholics, by articles and capitulation in this kingdom, charged with, and equally liable to the payment of so much of the said

ſaid debts, as the ſaid Lord Lucan, upon ſtating accounts with the ſaid John Brown, ſhall certify under his hand, that the effects taken from the ſaid Brown amount unto; which accompt is to be ſtated, and the balance certified by the ſaid Lord Lucan in one and twenty days after the date hereof:

For the true performance hereof, we have hereunto ſet our hands,

Present,	CHAR. PORTER.
SCRAVENMORE.	THOS. CONINGSBY.
H. MACCAY.	Bar. DE GINCKLE.
T. TALMASH.	

AND whereas the ſaid city of Limerick hath been ſince, in purſuance of the ſaid articles, ſurrendered unto us. Now know ye, that we having conſidered of the ſaid articles, are graciouſly pleaſed hereby to declare, *that we do for us, our heirs, and ſucceſſors, as far as in us lies, ratify and confirm the ſame, and every clauſe, matter, and thing therein contained.*— And as to ſuch parts thereof, for which an act of Parliament ſhall be found to be neceſſary, we ſhall recommend the ſame to be made good by Parliament, and ſhall give our royal aſſent to any bill or bills that ſhall be paſſed by our two houſes of Parliament to that purpoſe. And whereas it appears unto us, that it was agreed between the parties to the ſaid articles, that after the words, Limerick, Clare, Kerry, Cork, Mayo, or any of them, in the ſecond of the ſaid articles, the words following, viz. " And all ſuch as are " under their protection in the ſaid counties," ſhould be inſerted, and be part of the ſaid articles. Which

Which words having been casually omitted by the writer, the omission was not discovered till after the said articles were signed, but was taken notice of before the second town was surrendered: and that our said justices and general, or one of them, did promise that the said clause should be made good, it being within the intention of the capitulation, and inserted in the foul draft thereof. Our further will and pleasure is, and we do hereby ratify and confirm the said omitted words, viz. "And all such as are under their protection in the said counties," hereby for us, our heirs and successors, ordaining and declaring, that all and every person and persons therein concerned, shall and may have, receive, and enjoy the benefit thereof, in such and the same manner, as if the said words had been inserted in their proper place, in the said second article; any omission, defect, or mistake in the said second article, in any wise notwithstanding. Provided always, and our will and pleasure is, that these our letters patents shall be enrolled in our court of Chancery, in our said kingdom of Ireland, within the space of one year next ensuing. In witness, &c. witness ourself at Westminster, the twenty-fourth day of February, anno regni regis & reginæ Gulielmi & Mariæ quarto per breve de privato sigillo. Nos autem tenorem premissor. predict. Ad requisitionem attornat. general. domini regis & dominæ reginæ pro regno Hiberniæ. Duximus exemplificand. per presentes. In cujus rei testimonium has literas nostras fieri fecimus patentes. Testibus nobis ipsis apud Westmon. quinto die Aprilis, annoq. regni eorum quarto.

BRIDGES.

Examinat. per nos	S. Keck. Lacon Wm. Childe.	In Cancel. Magistros

MILITARY ARTICLES agreed upon between the Baron de Ginckle, Lieutenant-General and Commander in Chief of the English army, on the one ſide.

And the Lieutenant-Generals De Uſſoon and De Teſſe, Commanders in Chief of the Iriſh army, on the other; and the General Officers hereunto ſubſcribing.

I. THAT all perſons, without any exceptions, of what quality or condition ſoever, that are willing to leave the kingdom of Ireland, ſhall have free liberty to go to any country beyond the ſeas (England and Scotland excepted) where they think fit, with their families, houſehold-ſtuff, plate, and jewels.

II. That all general officers, colonels, and generally all other officers of horſe, dragoons, and foot-guards, troopers, dragooners, ſoldiers of all kinds that are in any garriſon, place, or poſt, now in the hands of the Iriſh, or encamped in the counties of Cork, Clare, and Kerry, as alſo thoſe called Rapparees, or volunteers, that are willing to go beyond ſeas as aforeſaid, ſhall have free leave to embark themſelves wherever the ſhips are that are appointed to tranſport them, and to come in whole bodies as they are now compoſed, or in parties, companies, or otherwiſe, without having any impediment, directly or indirectly.

III. That all perſons above-mentioned, that are willing to leave Ireland and go into France, ſhall have leave to declare it at the times and places hereafter mentioned, viz. the troops in Limerick, on Tueſday next in Limerick; the horſe at their camp on Wedneſday,

day, and the other forces that are difperfed in the counties of Clare, Kerry, and Cork, on the 8th inftant, and on none other, before Monfieur Tameron, the French intendant, and Colonel Withers; and after fuch delaration is made, the troops that will go into France muft remain under the command and difcipline of their officers that are to conduct them thither; and deferters of each fide fhall be given up, and punifhed accordingly.

IV. That all Englifh and Scotch officers that ferve now in Ireland, fhall be included in this capitulation, as well for the fecurity of their eftates and goods in England, Scotland, and Ireland, (if they are willing to remain here), as for paffing freely into France, or any other country to ferve.

V. That all the general French officers, the intendant, the engineers, the commiffaries at war, and of the artillery, the treafurer, and other French officers, ftrangers, and all others whatfoever, that are in Sligo, Rofs, Clare, or in the army, or that do trade or commerce, or are otherways employed in any kind of ftation or condition, fhall have free leave to pafs into France, or any other country, and fhall have leave to fhip themfelves, with all their horfes, equipage, plate, papers, and all their effects whatever; and that General Ginckle will order paffports for them, convoys, and carriages, by land and water, to carry them fafe from Limerick to the fhips where they fhall be embarked, without paying any thing for the faid carriages, or to thofe that are employed therein, with their horfes, cars, boats, and fhallops

VI. That if any of the aforefaid equipages, merchandize, horfes, money, plate, or other moveables, or houfehold-ftuff belonging to the faid Irifh troops, or to the French officers, or other particular perfons whatfoever, be robbed, deftroyed, or taken away by the troops of the faid General, the faid General will order it to be reftored, or payment to be made according to the value that is given in upon oath by the perfon fo robbed or plundered: and the faid Irifh troops to be tranfported as aforefaid: and all other perfons belonging to them, are to obferve good order in their march and quarters, and fhall reftore whatever they fhall take from the country, or make reftitution for the fame.

VII. That to facilitate the tranfporting the faid troops, the General will furnifh fifty fhips, each fhip's burthen two hundred tons; for which, the perfons to be tranfported fhall not be obliged to pay, and twenty more, if there fhall be occafion, without their paying for them; and if any of the faid fhips fhall be of leffer burthen, he will furnifh more in number to countervail; and alfo give two men of war to embark the principal officers, and ferve for a convoy to the veffels of burthen.

VIII. That a commiffary fhall be immediately fent to Cork to vifit the tranfport fhips, and what condition they are in for failing: and that as foon as they are ready, the troops to be tranfported fhall march with all convenient fpeed, the neareft way, in order to embark there: and if there fhall be any more men to be tranfported than can be carried off in the faid fifty fhips, the reft fhall quit the Englifh town of Limerick, and march

to

to ſuch quarters as ſhall be appointed for them, convenient for their tranſportation, where they ſhall remain till the other twenty ſhips be ready, which are to be in a month; and may embark on any French ſhip that may come in the mean time.

IX. That the ſaid ſhips ſhall be furniſhed with forage for horſe, and all neceſſary proviſions to ſubſiſt the officers, troops, dragoons, and ſoldiers, and all other perſons that are ſhipped to be tranſported into France; which proviſions ſhall be paid for as ſoon as all are diſembarked at Breſt or Nantz, upon the coaſt of Brittany, or any other port of France they can make.

X. And to ſecure the return of the ſaid ſhips (the danger of the ſeas excepted) and payment for the ſaid proviſions, ſufficient hoſtages ſhall be given.

XI. That the garriſons of Clare-caſtle, Roſs, and all other foot that are in garriſons in the counties of Clare, Cork, and Kerry, ſhall have the advantage of this preſent capitulation; and ſuch part of thoſe garriſons as deſign to go beyond ſeas, ſhall march out with their arms, baggage, drums beating, ball in mouth, match lighted at both ends, and colours flying, with all the proviſions, and half the ammunition that is in the ſaid garriſons, and join the horſe that march to be tranſported; or if then there is not ſhipping enough for the body of foot that is to be next tranſported after the horſe, General Ginckle will order that they be furniſhed with carriages for that purpoſe, and what proviſions they ſhall want in their march, they paying for the ſaid proviſions, or elſe that they may take it out of their own magazines.

XII. That all the troops of horſe and dragoons, that are in the counties of Cork, Kerry, and Clare, ſhall alſo have the benefit of this capitulation; and that ſuch as will paſs into France, ſhall have quarters given them in the counties of Clare and Kerry, apart from the troops that are commanded by General Ginckle, until they can be ſhipped; and within their quarters they ſhall pay for every thing, except forage and paſture for their horſes, which ſhall be furniſhed gratis.

XIII. Thoſe of the garriſon of Sligo that are joined to the Iriſh army, ſhall have the benefit of this capitulation; and orders ſhall be ſent to them that are to convey them up, to bring them hither to Limerick the ſhorteſt way

XIV. The Iriſh may have liberty to tranſport nine hundred horſe, including horſes for the officers, which ſhall be tranſported gratis: and as for the troopers that ſtay behind, they ſhall diſpoſe of themſelves as they ſhall think fit, giving up their horſes and arms to ſuch perſons as the General ſhall appoint.

XV. It ſhall be permitted to thoſe that are appointed to take care for the ſubſiſtence of the horſe, that are willing to go into France, to buy hay and corn at the King's rates wherever they can find it, in the quarters that are aſſigned for them, without any let or moleſtation, and to carry all neceſſary proviſions out of the city of Limerick; and for this purpoſe, the General will furniſh convenient carriages for them to the places where they ſhall be embarked.

XVI. It

XVI. It ſhall be lawful to make uſe of the hay preſerved in the ſtores of the county of Kerry, for the horſes that ſhall be embarked; and if there be not enough, it ſhall be lawful to buy hay and oats whereever it ſhall be found, at the King's rates.

XVII. That all priſoners of war, that were in Ireland the 28th of September, ſhall be ſet at liberty on both ſides; and the General promiſes to uſe his endeavours, that thoſe that are in England and Flanders ſhall be ſet at liberty alſo.

XVIII. The General will cauſe proviſions and medicines to be furniſhed to the ſick and wounded officers, troopers, dragoons, and ſoldiers of the Iriſh army, that cannot paſs into France at the firſt embarkment; and after they are cured, will order them ſhips to paſs into France, if they are willing to go.

XIX. That at the ſigning hereof, the General will ſend a ſhip expreſs to France; and that beſides, he will furniſh two ſmall ſhips of thoſe that are now in the river of Limerick, to tranſport two perſons into France that are to be ſent to give notice of this treaty; and that the commanders of the ſaid ſhips ſhall have orders to put aſhore at the next port of France where they ſhall make.

XX. That all thoſe of the ſaid troops, officers, and others, of what character ſoever, that would paſs into France, ſhall not be ſtopped upon the account of debt, or any other pretext.

XXI. If, after ſigning this preſent treaty, and before the arrival of the fleet, a French packet-boat, or other tranſport-ſhip, ſhall arrive from France in any other part of Ireland, the General will order a paſſport, not only for ſuch as muſt go on board the ſaid ſhips, but to the ſhips to come to the neareſt port to the place where the troops to be tranſported ſhall be quartered.

XXII. That after the arrival of the ſaid fleet, there ſhall be free communication and paſſage between it and the quarters of the above-ſaid troops; and eſpecially, for all thoſe that have paſſes from the chief Commanders of the ſaid fleet, or from Monſ. Tameron the intendant.

XXIII. In conſideration of the preſent capitulation, the two towns of Limerick ſhall be delivered and put into the hands of the General, or any other perſon he ſhall appoint, at the time and days hereafter ſpecified, viz. the Iriſh town, except the magazines and hoſpital, on the day of the ſigning of theſe preſent articles; and as for the Engliſh town, it ſhall remain, together with the iſland, and the free paſſage of Thomond-bridge, in the hands of thoſe of the Iriſh army that are now in the garriſon, or that ſhall hereafter come from the counties of Cork, Clare, Kerry, Sligo, and other places above-mentioned, until there ſhall be convenience found for their tranſportation.

XXIV. And to prevent all diſorders that may happen between the garriſon that the General ſhall place in the Iriſh town, which ſhall be delivered to him, and the Iriſh troopers that ſhall remain in the Engliſh town

and

and the iſland, which they may do, until the troops to be embarked on the firſt fifty ſhips ſhall be gone for France, and no longer; they ſhall entrench themſelves on both ſides, to hinder the communication of the ſaid garriſons; and it ſhall be prohibited on both ſides, to offer any thing that is offenſive; and the parties offending ſhall be puniſhed on either ſide.

XXV. That it ſhall be lawful for the ſaid garriſon to march out all at once, or at different times, as they can be embarked, *with arms, baggage, drums beating, match lighted at both ends, bullet in mouth, colours flying, ſix braſs guns, ſuch as the beſieged will chuſe, two mortar-pieces, and half the ammunition that is now in the magazines of the ſaid place;* and for this purpoſe an inventory of all the ammunition in the garriſon ſhall be made in the preſence of any perſon that the General ſhall appoint, the next day after theſe preſent articles ſhall be ſigned.

XXVI. All the magazines of proviſions ſhall remain in the hands of thoſe that are now employed to take care of the ſame, for the ſubſiſtence of thoſe of the Iriſh army that will paſs into France: and if there ſhall not be ſufficient in the ſtores, for the ſupport of the ſaid troops, whilſt they ſtay in this kingdom, and are croſſing the ſeas, that upon giving up an account of their numbers, the General will furniſh them with ſufficient proviſions at the King's rates; and that there ſhall be a free market at Limerick, and other quarters, where the ſaid troops ſhall be; and in caſe any proviſion ſhall remain in the magazines of Limerick when the town ſhall be given up, it ſhall be valued, and the price deducted

ducted out of what is to be paid for the provisions to be furnished to the troops on ship-board.

XXVII. That there shall be a cessation of arms at land, as also at sea, with respect to the ships, whether English, Dutch, or French, designed for the transportation of the said troops, until they shall be returned to their respective harbours; and that, on both sides, they shall be furnished with sufficient passports both for ships and men; and if any sea-commander, or captain of a ship, or any officer, trooper, dragoon, soldier, or any other person, shall act contrary to this cessation, the persons so acting shall be punished on either side, and satisfaction shall be made for the wrong that is done; and officers shall be sent to the mouth of the river of Limerick, to give notice to the commanders of the English and French fleets of the present conjuncture, that they may observe the cessation of arms accordingly.

XXVIII. That for the security of the execution of this present capitulation, and of each article therein contained, the besieged shall give the following hostages —— and the General shall give ——.

XXIX. If before this capitulation is fully executed, there happens any change in the government, or command of the army, which is now commanded by General Ginckle; all those that shall be appointed to command the same, shall be obliged to observe and execute what is specified in these articles, or cause it to be executed punctually, and shall not act contrary on any account.

Oct. 19. BARON DE GINCKLE.

If this treaty is only confidered according to thofe rules of common morality, which influence the conduct of man to man; if, in proportion to the great advantages which England derived from it, fhe was bound to conftrue it with liberality, as well as to execute it with good faith; then the Irifh Catholics muft be confidered as placed by it in a fituation of complete equality with their Proteftant countrymen. The free exercife of their religion was granted in the moft unqualified manner: Security of property was as fully confirmed to them. In regard to perfonal fecurity, they were pardoned all mifdemeanours whatfoever of which they had been guilty, and were reftored to all the rights, liberties, privileges, and immunities, which, by the laws of the land, and cuftoms, conftitutions, and native birthright, they, any, and every of them, were equally with every other of their fellow-fubjects entitled to.* The practice of the feveral trades or profeffions was fecured to them. They were allowed the ufe of arms, fome of them fpecially, but all of them in confequence of no limitation or exception to the contrary; and they were left at liberty to vote for members of Par-

 liament,

* Sir Theobald Butler's fpeech, vide Appendix, No. I.

liament, and to ſit in Parliament. The laws, even, which were in force againſt the Catholics when the treaty took place, ought, according to the firſt article, to have been repealed;† becauſe their

* The articles of Limerick were ſigned by De Ginckle on the 3d of October, 1691. The Engliſh Parliament that paſſed the act of 3d William and Mary, c. 2. by which Iriſh peers and members of Parliament were firſt required to take the oath of ſupremacy, met on the 22d October, 1691. According to the conſtitution of Ireland, as granted by Henry 2d, and confirmed in 1782, this act of 3d William and Mary, c. 2. was not binding in Ireland; and, though the Catholics ſubmitted to it, they were not legally excluded from Parliament till the 22d year of his preſent Majeſty's reign.

† Theſe laws were, 1ſt. An act againſt the authority of the See of Rome. It enacts, that no perſon ſhall attribute any juriſdiction to the See of Rome; that the perſon offending to be ſubject to a premunire; and, that all who have any office from the King, every perſon entering into orders, or taking a degree in the Univerſity, ſhall take the oath of ſupremacy.

2d. An act reſtoring to the Crown the antient juriſdiction over the State, eccleſiaſtical and ſpiritual. It likewiſe enacts that every eccleſiaſtical perſon, every perſon accepting office, ſhall take the oath of ſupremacy.

3d. An act for the uniformity of common prayer. It enacts, that every perſon, having no lawful excuſe to be abſent, ſhall, every Sunday, reſort to ſome place of worſhip of the eſtabliſhed Church, or forfeit 12d.

4th. An act, by which the Chancellor may appoint a guardian to the child of a Catholic.

5th.

their Majesties engaged, by this article, to obtain for the Catholics such further security, in respect to the exercise of their religion, *as might preserve them from any disturbance on account of that religion.* It is impossible for any other fair construction to be given of this article, than that which is here given. It would be beneath the dignity, and wholly inconsistent with that character for good faith, of which it has always been the pride of England to boast, to attempt to apply any other meaning to it. No doubt there are those who would wish to act, on all occasions, towards the Catholics, according to that system of perverted morality which the powerful always impose on the weak; but, so long as the true principles of justice shall have their due influence, the majority of mankind can never consider this first article of the treaty of Limerick in any other light, than as a

 complete

5th, An act, by which no Catholic schoolmaster can teach in a private house without a license from the ordinary of his diocese, and taking the oath of supremacy.

6th, The new rules, by which no person can be admitted into any corporation without taking the oath of supremacy.

This statement is taken from the Report of the Committee of the House of Commons, appointed, in 1697, to consider what penal laws were then in force against the Catholics.—*Com. Jour. v.* 2.

complete and perpetual exemption of the Irifh Catholics from all political and religious difqualification on account of their religion. This treaty has been very accurately defcribed as the great charter of the civil and religious liberty of the Catholics;* and though not hitherto obferved as fuch by the Englifh Government, the Catholics have a right (which time cannot efface nor perfidy deftroy) to recur to its ftipulations; and if an Englifh Government *can* act with juftice towards them, their appeal will not for ever be made in vain.

Though William had bound himfelf by this treaty to call a Parliament as foon as his affairs would admit, and to obtain from it the ratification of the treaty, he diffolved the firft Parliament of his reign, which had met on the 5th October, 1692, in September, 1693, without propofing to them any fuch meafure. He was further guilty of a want of attention to his engagement, by not fummoning another Parliament till the 27th April, 1695; and, when this Parliament did meet, he feems to have entirely forgotten, that his own faith,

* Smollet.

faith, and the faith of the English nation, was plighted to the Catholics by a solemn treaty; for, instead of recommending to them, in the speech of his Lord Deputy, to proceed to confirm the articles of Limerick, he told them that he was intent upon the great work of a firm settlement of Ireland upon a *Protestant* interest.* The Parliament were not backward in promoting his object. They first of all passed an act to deprive the Catholics of the means of educating their children either at home or abroad, and of the privilege of being guardians either of their own or of any other person's children.† Then they passed an act to disarm the Catholics,‡ another to banish their priests,

* Comm. Journal, 2. 279.

† 7th W. III. c. 4. of this act, Mr. Burke says, "Whilst this restraint upon foreign and domestic education was part of a horrible and impious system of servitude, the members were well fitted to the body. To render men patient, under a deprivation of all the rights of human nature, every thing which could give them a knowledge or feeling of those rights was rationally forbidden. To render humanity fit to be insulted, it was fit that it should be degraded. Indeed, I have ever thought the prohibition of the means of improving our rational nature, to be the worst species of tyranny that the insolence and perverseness of mankind ever dared to exercise." —*Letter to a Peer in Ireland.*

‡ 7th W. III. c. 5.

priefts,* and, ftrange as it may appear, they then thought proper in the year 1697 to pafs an act to *confirm* the articles of Limerick.†

Of this act it is to be obferved, in the firft place, that the very title of it is a proof of its injuftice; for it is ftyled "an act for the confirmation *of articles*," and not, as it ought to be, "of *the* articles" made at the furrender of Limerick."

The preamble affords further evidence of the intention of the framers of it to evade its proper object. It runs "That the faid articles, or *fo much of them* as may confift with the fafety and welfare of your Majefty's fubjects of this kingdom, may be confirmed," &c.

But the whole act goes to convict the Parliament, (and as this Parliament was completely under the controul of the Lord Deputy,)‡ even William

* 9th William III. c. 1.

† 9th William III. c. 2.

‡ "He (Lord Capel, the Lord Deputy) undertook to model a Parliament in fuch a manner, that they fhould comply with all the demands of the Miniftry, and he fucceeded in his endeavours, by making fuch arbitrary changes in offices as beft fuited his purpofe.—*Smollet Hift.* 232.

"He

William himſelf, of groſs injuſtice towards the Catholics. For the firſt article of the treaty is wholly omitted, which guarantees to the Catholics the free exerciſe of their religion, and an exemption from all diſturbance on account of it; and each clauſe of the act has the effect of limiting the terms of the other articles, and depriving the Catholics of the benefit of them, inſtead of ratifying and confirming them.

The firſt clauſe, which refers at once to the ſecond article, explains who are entitled to the benefit of it, and the rights conferred upon them; aſſuming as a fact, for which there could be no foundation, that this article required explanation. With reſpect to the perſons entitled to the benefit of the treaty, a moſt remarkable difference occurs between the words of the ſecond article, and thoſe of this clauſe in deſcribing *them*. In the ratification of the treaty by William, there is the following paſſage: "And whereas it appears to us, that it was agreed between the parties to the ſaid articles,

" He carried the projects of the Crown in Parliament, and was recommended as an excellent governor, in a ſpecial addreſs ſent by the Commons to the King."—*Macpherſon's Hiſt.* 2. 94.

articles, that after the words Limerick, Clare, Kerry, Cork, and Mayo, or any of them, in the ſecond of the ſaid articles, the words following, viz. "And all ſuch as are under their protection in the ſaid counties," ſhould be inſerted and be part of the ſaid article; "Our further will and pleaſure is, and we do ratify and confirm the ſaid omitted words." Theſe words, according even to the ſtrict letter of the article, extended the benefit of the treaty to the whole Catholic population of theſe counties, which certainly was the object of the treaty, as it may be collected from the preamble to it, in which it is ſtated that the Iriſh generals acted in behalf of the Iriſh inhabitants of theſe counties. But in this clauſe of the act of Parliament to *confirm* the treaty, theſe words are omitted, and therefore the benefit of the treaty is limited, by this explanatory and confining act, to the Iriſh army and the inhabitants of the city of Limerick, and a few more garriſon towns: a limitation in every reſpect moſt perfidious, and wholly unjuſtifiable upon any plea of ambiguity in the language of the article, even if ſuch a plea could for a moment be allowed.

With reſpect to the rights conferred by the

ſecond

ſecond article, this clauſe affords a ſtriking proof of the paltry ſubterfuges to which the Legiſlature of that day could have recourſe in order to defeat the ends of juſtice, and to oppreſs the Catholics. The ſecond article declares that all thoſe compriſed in the treaty, "ſhall hold, poſſeſs "and enjoy all and every their eſtates of free-"hold and inheritance; and all the rights, titles "and intereſts, privileges and immunities, which "they every or any of them hold, enjoyed, or "were rightfully and lawfully entitled to in the "reign of King Charles II." The clauſe of the act correſponds with the article, except in theſe moſt material points; after the word "inheritance:" the ſtop, inſtead of being a ſemicolon, as it was in the original treaty, is altered to a comma; and after the words "privileges and immunities," the words "to the ſaid eſtates" are inſerted; and thus the meaning of the ſecond article is wholly altered, and the words, "rights, privileges and immunities," made to refer to the eſtates of the Catholics, inſtead of to their perſons and liberties, to which only by the original article they can refer. If any authority were wanting to maintain this conſtruction, a very unqueſtionable one may be adduced from the ſpeech of Sir

Theobald Butler, before alluded to, who was in Limerick when it surrendered, and was the person employed to draw up the treaty.

This act for *confirming* the treaty, wholly omits that part of the second article, which guarantees to the Catholics the exercise of their several trades and professions. It also omits the fourth article. It limits the benefit of the indemnity granted by the sixth article to a period subsequent to the 10th of April, 1689, and enables all persons, who suffered any injuries between the 5th of November, 1688, and this period, to bring their actions for the same until the 1st of September, 1691, by declaring that the commencement of the war referred to in the article was the 10th of April, 1689, and not the 5th of November, 1688, and it omits the 7th, 8th, 9th, and 10th articles. Being in short an act, that, under the name of conferring favours on the Catholics, really placed them in a worse condition, than that in which they were before it passed into a law.

The other acts of this reign, relating to the Catholics, are an act to prevent Protestants from intermarrying with Papists,* and an act to prevent them

* 9th William III. c. 3.

them from being ſolicitors.* A clauſe was introduced in an act for the preſervation of game, prohibiting Papiſts from being employed as game-keepers.†

How it is poſſible to defend William and his miniſters from the charge of having acted with perfidy towards the Catholics, it is not eaſy to diſcover. That they were guilty of violating the treaty no one can deny. The excuſe that has been made for William, that he was obliged to ſubmit to the power of the anti-catholic party, may eaſily be proved to be a mere pretext. In the firſt place, the Parliament which paſſed theſe laws was under the controul of William; beſides he encouraged them, by a ſpeech from the throne, to ſtrengthen the Proteſtant intereſt. The preamble of the act for confirming the treaty, ſtates they were recommended by William to confirm only a part of the articles. But why did he not refuſe his conſent to theſe laws, on the ground of their being contrary to his ſolemn engagements to the Catholics? He had exerciſed this prerogative in the caſe of one Scotch,‡ and of one

 Engliſh

* 10th William III. c. 13.

† 10th William III. c. 8.

‡ For excluding from any public truſt all ſuch as had been concerned in the encroachments of the late reign.

Englifh bill.* But even this extremity might have been avoided, becaufe the laws of Poynings required that every bill fhould be approved by the King and Council of England before it could pafs the Houfe of Commons; and, if a bill was exceptionable, by withholding their approbation, a very common proceeding, it fell of courfe to the ground.

But if William and his minifters were guilty of perfidy towards the Catholics, his fucceffor far outftripped him. Nor has any fucceeding prince been free from the blame of having been an acceffary to his crime, in proportion as they have neglected or refufed to repeal thofe penal laws, which are fo many glaring violations of the treaty of Limerick, which are a fcandal to the boafted good faith of the Englifh nation, and a mockery of that equitable religion, whofe precepts are founded upon the pureft principles of juftice and humanity.

ANNE.

* Concerning free and impartial proceedings in Parliament.

ANNE.

On the 4th of March, 1704, the royal aſſent was given to the *act to prevent the further growth of popery;* being the firſt of theſe two famous acts, which have moſt deſervedly been termed by Mr. Burke, the ferocious acts of Anne.

By the third clauſe of this act the popiſh father, though he may have acquired his eſtate by deſcent from a long line of anceſtors, or by his own purchaſe, is deprived of the power, in caſe his eldeſt ſon, or any other ſon, becomes a Proteſtant, to ſell, mortgage, or otherwiſe diſpoſe of it, or to leave out of it any portions or legacies.

By the 4th clauſe, the popiſh father is debarred, under a penalty of 500l. from being a guardian to, or from having the cuſtody of his own children; but if the child, though ever ſo young, pretends to be a Proteſtant, it is to be taken from its own father, and put into the hands of a Proteſtant relation.

The 5th clauſe provides that no Proteſtant ſhall marry a Papiſt, having an eſtate in Ireland, either in or out of the kingdom.

The

The 6th clauſe renders Papiſts incapable of purchaſing any manors, tenements, hereditaments, or any rents or profits ariſing out of the ſame, or of holding any leaſe of lives, or other leaſe whatever, for any term exceeding 31 years. Even with reſpect to this advantage reſtrictions were impoſed on them, one of which was, that if a farm produced a profit greater than one-third of the amount of the rent, the right in it was immediately to ceaſe, and to paſs over entirely to the firſt Proteſtant who ſhould diſcover the rate of profit.

The 7th clauſe deprives Papiſts of ſuch inheritance, deviſe, gift, remainder or truſt, of any lands, tenements or hereditaments, of which any Proteſtant was, or ſhould be ſeized in fee ſimple, abſolute or fee tail, which, by the death of ſuch Proteſtant, or his wife, ought to have deſcended to his ſon or other iſſue in tail, being Papiſts, and makes them deſcend to the neareſt Proteſtant relation, as if the Popiſh heir and other Popiſh relations were dead.

By the 10th clauſe, the eſtate of a Papiſt, for want of a Proteſtant heir, is to be divided, ſhare and ſhare alike, among all his ſons; for want of ſons, among his daughters; and, for want of daughters,

daughters, among the collateral kindred of the father.

By the 15th clauſe, no perſon ſhall be exempt from the penalties of this act, that ſhall not take and ſubſcribe the oath and declaration required by this act to be taken.

By the 16th clauſe, all perſons whatſoever who ſhall receive any office, civil and military, ſhall take and ſubſcribe the oath and declaration required to be taken by the Engliſh act of 3d Wm. and Mary; and alſo the oath of abjuration required to be taken by another Engliſh act of 1ſt Anne; and alſo ſhall receive the ſacrament.*

The 23d clauſe provides, that no Papiſt, except under particular conditions, ſhall dwell in Limerick or Galway.

The

* Upon this clauſe of the bill Biſhop Burnet makes the following obſervations: "A clauſe was added (in England) which they (the Roman Catholics) hoped would hinder its being accepted in Ireland. The matter was carried on ſo ſecretly, that it was known to none but thoſe who were at the Council, till the news of it came from Ireland, upon its being ſent thither.—It was hoped, by thoſe who got this clauſe added to the bill, that thoſe in Ireland, who promoted it, would be leſs fond of it when it had ſuch a weight hung to it." *Hiſt. v. 2. p.* 214.

This clauſe has ſince been called the Sacramental Teſt, the firſt impoſed on diſſenters in Ireland. It was repealed without any oppoſition in the Seſſions of 1782.

The 24th, that no perſons ſhall vote at elections without taking the oaths of allegiance and abjuration.

And the 25th clauſe, that all advowſons poſſeſſed by Papiſts ſhall be veſted in her Majeſty.

The Catholics, who had ſubmitted in ſilence to all the unjuſt tranſgreſſions of the laſt reign, felt it neceſſary, when this act was firſt brought before Parliament, to uſe their utmoſt exertions to prevent it from paſſiing into a law. They, however, appealed in vain to the Engliſh Cabinet to reſpect the ſolemn engagements of the treaty of Limerick, and were obliged to have recourſe to a petition to the Iriſh Parliament.

Sir Theobald Butler was heard, as counſel for the petitioners, at the bar of the Houſe of Commons, on the 22d February, 1703: He ſtated, "that the bill would render null and void the ar-"ticles of Limerick; that thoſe articles had been "granted for the valuable conſideration of the "ſurrender of that garriſon, at a time when the "Catholics had the ſword in their hand, and were "in a condition to hold out much longer; and

"when

" when they had it in their power to demand and
" make ſuch terms as might be for their own fu-
" ture liberty, ſafety, and ſecurity: That the al-
" lowing of the terms contained in theſe articles
" were highly advantageous to the government
" to which they ſubmitted, as well for uniting
" the people that were then divided, quieting
" and ſettling the diſtractions and diſorders of
" this miſerable kingdom, as for the other advan-
" tages which the government would thereby
" reap in its own affairs, both at home and
" abroad, when its enemies were ſo powerful,
" both by ſea and land, as to render the peace
" and ſettlement of theſe countries a circumſtance
" of great uncertainty: That theſe articles were
" ratified by their late Majeſties, for themſelves,
" their heirs, and ſucceſſors, and the public faith
" thereby plighted to all thoſe compriſed in theſe
" articles, in the moſt binding manner it was poſ-
" ſible for faith to be plighted, and than which
" nothing could be more ſacred and ſolemn: That,
" therefore, to violate and break thoſe articles
" would, on the contrary, be the greateſt injuſtice
" poſſible for any one people of the whole world

"to inflict upon another, and contrary to both "the laws of God and man." He then proceeded to shew that the clauses of the bill which take away from Catholics the right to purchase, bequeath, sell, and inherit estates, were infringements of the 2d article of the treaty: That the 9th clause of the bill, imposing upon Catholics new oaths, was another manifest breach of the articles, for that, by the 9th article, no oath is to be administered to, nor imposed upon such Catholics as should submit to government, but the oath of allegiance, appointed by an act made in England in the first year of the reign of their late Majesties; that the clauses for prohibiting Catholics from residing in Limerick or Galway, from voting at elections without taking certain new oaths, and from possessing advowsons, were likewise infringements of the treaty. "For if," concludes Sir Theobald Butler, "there was no law in force in "the reign of Charles II. against these things, as "there certainly was not, and if the Roman "Catholics of this kingdom have not since for- "feited their right to the laws that then were in "force, as for certain they have not, then, with "humble

"humble submission, all the aforesaid clauses, "and matters contained in this bill, entitled, *An* "*Act to prevent the further growth of Popery*, are "directly against the plain words and true interest "and meaning of the said articles, and a violation "of the public faith."*

In consequence of the passing of this act, and of those other acts which were passed of a similar tendency in the last reign, the Catholics were deprived of all those privileges and immunities, which they trusted had been secured in consequence of a King of England having bound himself, his heirs and successors, to fulfil the conditions of the treaty of Limerick. In place of being the free subjects of a prince, from whom they were taught to expect only justice and mercy, they were made the slaves of every one, even of the very meanest, of their Protestant countrymen. They saw the English government, on whom they had claims for protection against their own parliament, directing its fanatic councils and confirming its crimes. By the treaty of Limerick they were

 left

* Vid. App. No. 1. for the Speech at length of Sir Toby Butler.

left at liberty to educate, and to act as guardians to their own children: by the penal laws they neither can send them to be educated abroad, or have them educated at home, or be guardians to their own, or the children of any other persons.

By the treaty of Limerick, the free exercise of their religion was guaranteed to them. By the penal laws their priests are banished, hanged if they returned home, and their chapels shut up.

By the treaty of Limerick, their noblemen and gentlemen were specially allowed the privilege of wearing arms, and the whole body were equally entitled to the same privilege, because, when it was executed, no law existed to the contrary. By the penal laws, no Catholic is permitted to have the use of arms, except a very few even of those who were specially comprized in the treaty.

By the treaty of Limerick, Catholics might intermarry with Protestants. By the penal laws this privilege is removed.

By

By the treaty of Limerick, the profeſſion of the law was open to them; by theſe laws it is taken from them.

By the treaty of Limerick, the Catholics could purchaſe, ſell, bequeath, and inherit landed property. By the penal laws they can neither purchaſe, ſell, bequeath or inherit landed property, take annuities for lives ſecured on lands, or any longer leaſe of land than for 31 years; nor could they lend money on mortgage* or veſt it in public ſecurities.

By the treaty of Limerick, the Catholics were left in full enjoyment of every political franchiſe, except thoſe of holding offices under government, and of becoming members of corporations. By the penal laws, they can not vote at veſtries, ſerve on grand juries, act as conſtables, or as ſheriffs or under-ſheriffs, be magiſtrates, vote at elections, or ſit in parliament.†

By

* By a conſtruction of Lord Hardwicke.

† "The excluſion from the law, from grand juries, from ſheriffships and under-ſheriffships, as well as from freedom in any corporation, may ſubject them to dreadful hardſhips, as

By the treaty of Limerick, they were protected from being called upon to take any other oaths besides the oath of allegiance of the 1st William and Mary. By the penal laws they are required to take the oaths of abjuration and supremacy, and to subscribe declarations against the principal tenets of their religious faith.

By the treaty of Limerick, they were acknowledged as the free subjects of a British King; by the penal laws they are placed in the double capacity of slaves and enemies of their Protestant countrymen. Had they become mere slaves, they might have experienced some degree of humane treatment; but, as the policy which made them slaves, held them out at the same time as the natural

it may exclude them wholly from all that is beneficial, and expose them to all that is mischievous in a trial by jury. This was manifestly within my own observation, for I was three times in Ireland from the year 1760 to the year 1767, where I had sufficient means of information, concerning the inhuman proceedings (among which were many cruel murders, besides an infinity of outrages and oppressions, unknown before in a civilized age) which prevailed during that period, in consequence of a pretended conspiracy among Roman Catholics against the King's Government."—*Burke's Letter to a Peer of Ireland.*

ral and interested enemies of their masters, they were doomed to experience all the oppression of tyranny, without any of the chances, that other slaves enjoy, of their tyrants being merciful, from feeling their tyranny secure.

This statement will be sufficient to convince those who really form their political opinions upon moral and just principles, that the penal laws never should have been enacted; and that it is the duty of every upright statesman to promote the instant repeal of the whole of them: because it proves a solemn compact entered into between the Catholics and the English Government, and the breach of that contract by the English Government, notwithstanding the Catholics fulfilled their part of the agreement. That man must, indeed, be a most consummate hypocrite, who assumes to himself a pre-eminent character for virtue and morality, and who yet can gravely and zealously contribute to make perpetual the political disabilities of the Catholics, which were the base and perfidious means adopted by a wicked legislature to influence men's consciences by corrupt motives, and tempt and bribe them to apostacy.

As

As there are, however, no ſmall number of politicians who, though they would think it an edifying exhibition to ſee a Catholic conſigned to martyrdom (occaſionally), yet would be ſcandalized at the bare idea of breaking faith with him in any affair of barter, particularly if they had already received from him their conſideration, and that a valuable one; it will be neceſſary to make ſome further obſervations upon the violation of the treaty of Limerick, in order that no one may have a pretext on which he can eſcape the fair concluſion that ought to be drawn from what has been advanced, that the Engliſh government and nation are, at this day, bound to make good to the Catholics of Ireland the ſtipulations contained in that treaty. For, if ever there was an inſtance in which the conſideration that formed the baſis of a treaty ſhould have ſecured a liberal and a juſt fulfilment, it was the inſtance of this treaty of Limerick. In the courſe of the three campaigns during which the war laſted in Ireland, the Engliſh army had been defeated on ſeveral occaſions. In the North under Schomberg; before Athlone under Douglas; and before Limerick under

der William himſelf. The victory of the Boyne was the reſult of the perſonal feelings of James, not of any deficiency in the number of his army, or of any want of courage on their part. "Exchange Kings," ſaid the Iriſh officers, "and we will once more fight the battle." St. Ruth had won the battle of Aughrim, and had exclaimed, in an ecſtacy of joy, "Now will I drive the Engliſh to the walls of Dublin," at the moment the fatal ball ſtruck him.* And, at the time the garriſon of Limerick capitulated, the Iriſh army was in a condition to hold out at leaſt another campaign, with a good proſpect of being able to reſtore the fallen fortunes of James. The beſieging army had made no impreſſion on the principal part of the city; it was inferior in numbers to that of the garriſon; winter was faſt approaching, and at the very moment French ſuccours were on the coaſt:† yet all theſe advantages did the Iriſh army forego, in conſideration of the terms which were granted to them by the treaty of Limerick. On the other hand, in granting theſe terms, the Engliſh government and nation obtained advantages

H of

* Leland, B. 6. c. 7. † Note A. Appendix.

of the utmoſt importance. For ſo long as James had a powerful army in Ireland, and nearly one-half of the kingdom under his dominion, the great work of the revolution was neither accompliſhed or ſecured. The fair way, therefore, of judging of the value of the treaty of Limerick to England, is to conſider how far it contributed to promote this ineſtimable object. If the treaty of Limerick, in any degree, led to the eſtabliſhment of the revolution, the vaſt importance of this event ſhould have inclined the people of England to act with juſtice, at leaſt, towards the Catholics. But if their ſubmiſſion contributed eſſentially to crown the brilliant efforts of the friends of liberty with ſucceſs, then indeed the people of England ſhould have felt zealous to act towards the Catholics, not on a cold calculation of what was merely juſt on their part, but with that kindneſs with which we always regard thoſe who have promoted our proſperity, whether intentionally or not. That the ſubmiſſion of the Iriſh Catholics did ſo contribute to complete the revolution is plain, from the means which they poſſeſſed of continuing the war; from the opportunity it afforded William to bring his whole forces to bear againſt Louis; and

from

from the termination it fixed to the hopes and the confpiracies of the adherents of James in England. Yet, notwithftanding the great conceffions which the Catholics, on their part, made by their fubmiffion, in order to obtain the terms of the treaty of Limerick, and the great advantages which the Englifh nation, on the other hand, acquired by it, twelve years only elapfed before the Catholics were deprived of every right and privilege which was folemnly guaranteed to them by that treaty.

The only fpecies of juftification that could, under any circumftances, have been brought forward for acting in this manner towards the Catholics, would have been, the proof of the forfeiture, by mifconduct, of their right to the fulfilment of the treaty. That any thing which they did prior to the treaty, could have, in juftice, any influence on meafures paffed fubfequent to its taking place, is quite impoffible; becaufe the treaty admitted their acts to be thofe of open and honourable enemies, and fpecifically pardoned them.* As to their

* "The peculiar fituation of that country, (Ireland)," fays Macpherfon, "feems to have been overlooked in the conteft. The

their conduct afterwards, even their most inveterate and most unprincipled enemies did not charge them with a single transgression against the State, from the year 1691 to the year 1704, when the act to prevent the farther growth of Popery was passed. And it is very plain that no such charge could be maintained, from the paltry attempt that was made in Parliament to justify this act. It was said, "That the Papists had not demonstrated "how and where, since the making of the articles "of Limerick, they had addressed the Queen or "Government, when all other subjects were so "doing; and that any right, which they pre-"tended was to be taken from them by the bill, "was in their own power to remedy, by con-"forming,

The desertion, upon which the deprivation of James had been founded in England, had not existed in Ireland. The Lord Lieutenantcy had retained his allegiance. The government was uniformly continued under the name of the Prince, from whom the servants of the Crown had derived their commissions. James himself had, for more than 17 months, exercised the royal function in Ireland. He was certainly *de facto*, if not *de jure*, King. The rebellion of the Irish must, therefore, be founded on the supposition, that their allegiance is transferable by the Parliament of England. A speculative opinion can scarcely justify the punishment of a great majority of a people. The Irish ought to have been considered as enemies, rather than rebels."—*Hist. Great Britain.*

“ forming, as in prudence they ought to do; and “ that they ought not to blame any but them- “ ſelves.”* No circumſtance can poſſibly illuſtrate more clearly the innocence of the Catholics, and their loyalty and good conduct, from the treaty of Limerick to the paſſing of this act, than this mockery of juſtification; nor could any thing more diſtinctly bring to our underſtandings an accurate comprehenſion of the perfidy and baſeneſs of that government, and of that Parliament, which could adduce ſo ſilly an excuſe for ſuch ſtern and crafty oppreſſion.

Though the treaty of Limerick was now violated in every point, the ſpirit of perſecution was ſtill reſtleſs and unſatisfied. However great was the ingenuity of the legiſlators who produced that maſter-piece of oppreſſion, the act to prevent the farther growth of Popery, it was found that another act was ſtill wanting to explain and amend it. Such an act paſſed in the year 1709.†

The 1ſt clauſe provides, that no Papiſt ſhall be capable of taking any annuity for life.

The

* Debates on the Popery Laws, App. I. † 8th Anne, c. 3.

The following is the 3d claufe, every word of which is of value, in order to fhew the cruelty with which the unfortunate Catholics of Ireland have been oppreffed: " And, be it further enacted, " by the authority aforefaid, that where and as " often as any child or children of any Popifh " parent or parents hath or have heretofore pro- " feffed or conformed him, her, or themfelves, to " the Proteftant religion, as by law eftablifhed, " and enrolled in the High Court of Chancery a " certificate of the Bifhop of the diocefs in which " fhe or they fhall inhabit or refide, teftifying " his, her, or their being a Proteftant, and con- " forming him, her, or themfelves, to the Church " of Ireland, as by law eftablifhed, it fhall and " may be lawful for the High Court of Chan- " cery, upon a bill founded upon this act, to ob- " lige the faid Papift parent or parents to difcover " upon oath the full value of all his, her, or their " eftate, as well perfonal as real, clear, over and " above all real incumbrances and debts contract- " ed, bona fide, for valuable confideration, before " the enrolment of fuch certificate, and thereupon " to make fuch order for the fupport and mainte- " nance of fuch Proteftant child or children, by

" the

" the distribution of the said real and personal
" estate, to and among such Protestant child
" or children, for the present support of such
" Protestant child or children; and also to and
" for the portion or portions, and future mainte-
" nance or maintenances, of such Protestant child
" or children, after the decease of such Popish
" parent or parents, as the said court shall judge
" fit."

The 12th clause provides, that all converts in public employments, members of parliament, barristers, attornies, or officers of any courts of law, shall educate their children Protestants.

By the 14th clause, the Popish wife of a Papist, having power to make a jointure, conforming, shall, if she survives her husband, have such provision, not exceeding the power of her husband, to make a jointure, as the Chancellor shall adjudge.

By the 15th clause, the Popish wife of a Papist, not being otherwise provided for, conforming, shall have a proportion out of his chattels, not-

withstanding

withſtanding any will or voluntary diſpoſition, and the ſtat. 7th W. III. 6.

The 16th clauſe provides, that a Papiſt teaching ſchool publicly, or in a private houſe, or as uſher to a Proteſtant, ſhall be deemed and proſecuted as a Popiſh regular convict.

The 18th clauſe provides, that Popiſh prieſts, who ſhall be converted, ſhall receive 30l. per annum, to be levied and paid by Grand Juries.

The 20th clauſe provides, whimſically enough, for the reward of diſcovering Popiſh clergy and ſchoolmaſters, viz.

For diſcovering an archbiſhop, biſhop, vicar-general, or other perſon exerciſing any foreign eccleſiaſtical juriſdiction - - - -	£. 50 0 0
For diſcovering each regular clergyman, and each ſecular clergyman, not regiſtered - - -	20 0 0
For diſcovering each Popiſh ſchoolmaſter or uſher - -	£. 10 0 0

For

The 21st clause empowers two justices to summon any Papist of 18 years of age, and if he shall refuse to give testimony where and when he heard mass celebrated, and who and what persons were present at the celebration of it, and likewise touching the residence and abode of any priest or Popish schoolmaster, to commit him to jail, without bail, for 12 months, or until he shall pay 20l.

By the 25th clause, no priest can officiate except in the parish for which he is registered, by 2d Anne, c. 7.

The 30th clause provides for the discovery of all trusts agreed to be undertaken in favour of Papists; and enables any Protestant to file a bill in Chancery against any person concerned in any sale, lease, mortgage, or incumbrance, in trust for Papists, and to compel him to discover the same; and it further provides, that all issues to be tried in any action founded upon this act, shall be tried by none but known Protestants.

The 37th clause provides, that no Papist in trade, except in the linen trade, shall take more than two apprentices.

The following are the other acts passed in this reign concerning the Catholics.

An act to prevent Popish clergy from coming into the kingdom.*

An act for registering Popish clergy. By which all the Catholic clergy then in the kingdom were required to give in their names and places of abode at the next quarter sessions; by this act they are prohibited from employing curates.†

An act to amend this act. ‡

An act to explain and amend an act to prevent Papists being solicitors or sheriffs, &c.§

Clauses are introduced into this act by which Catholics were prevented from serving on grand juries; and by which, in trials upon any statute for strengthening the Protestant interest, the plaintiff might challenge a Papist, which challenge the judge was to allow. If absurdity could catch the attention

* 2d Anne, c. 3.

† 2d Anne, c. 7.

‡ 4th Anne, c. 2.

§ 6th Anne, c. 1.

attention where ferocity is ſo prominent, one might ſmile to ſee this code of Queen Anne, entitled, as it then was in all public documents, A Wiſe Syſtem for the Quieting and Settling of Ireland.

During all Queen Anne's reign, the inferior civil officers, by order of government, were inceſſantly haraſſing the Catholics, with oaths, impriſonments, and forfeitures, without any viſible cauſe but hatred of their religious profeſſion. In the year 1708, on the bare rumour of an intended invaſion of Scotland by the Pretender, 41 Roman Catholic noblemen and gentlemen were impriſoned in the caſtle of Dublin; and, when they were afterwards ſet at liberty, the government was ſo ſenſible of the wrong done to them, that it remitted their fees, amounting to 800l. A cuſtom that had exiſted, from time immemorial, for infirm men, women, and children, to make a pilgrimage every ſummer to a place called St. John's well, in the county of Meath, in hopes of obtaining relief from their ſeveral diſorders, by performing at it certain acts of penance and devotion, was deemed an object worthy of the ſerious conſideration of the Houſe of Commons; who accordingly paſſed a vote, that these sickly devotees "were assembled "in that place to the great hazard and danger of "the public peace, and safety of the kingdom." They also passed a vote, on the 17th March, 1705, "That all magistrates and other persons "whatsoever, who neglected or omitted to put "them (the penal laws) in due execution, were "betrayers of the liberties of the kingdom;"* and, in June 1705, they resolved, "That the "saying and hearing of mass, by persons who had "not taken the oath of abjuration, tended to ad-"vance the interest of the Pretender; and that "such judges and magistrates as wilfully neglected "to make diligent inquiry into, and to discover "such wicked practices, ought to be looked upon "as enemies to her Majesty's government."† And, upon another occasion, they resolved, "That "the prosecuting and informing against Papists "was an honourable service to the govern-"ment."‡

* Com. Jour. 3. 289. † Ib. 319. ‡ Ib. 319.

GEORGE

GEORGE I.

The following acts of Parliament were passed in this reign, for the purpose of strengthening the system which had been adopted by William and Anne, for preventing the growth of Popery.

An act to make the militia of this kingdom more useful.*

By the 11th and 12th clauses of this act, the horses of Papists may be seized for the militia.

By the 4th and 18th clauses, Papists are to pay double towards raising the militia.

By the 16th clause, Popish house-keepers in a city, are to find fit Protestant substitutes.

An act to restrain Papists from being high or petty constables, and for the better regulating the parish watches.†

An

* 2d G. I. c. 9.

† 2d G. I. c. 10.—This act expired in three years, and was not renewed.

An aſt for the more effectual preventing fraudulent conveyances, in order to multiply votes for electing members to ſerve in Parliament, &c.*

By the 7th clauſe of this act no Papiſt can vote at an election unleſs he takes the oaths of allegiance and *abjuration*.

An act for the better regulating the town of Galway, and for ſtrengthening the Proteſtant intereſt therein.†

An act for the better regulating the corporation of the city of Kilkenny, and ſtrengthening the Proteſtant intereſt therein.‡

An act by which Papiſts reſident in towns, who ſhall not provide a Proteſtant watchman to watch in their room, ſhall be ſubject to certain penalties.‖

By the 7th clauſe of this act, no Papiſt can vote at a veſtry.

Theſe

* 2d Geo. I. c. 19.

† 4th Geo. I. c. 15.

‡ 4th Geo. I. c. 16.

‖ 6th Geo. I. c. 10.

These acts of Parliament originated in the same spirit of persecution, which disgraced the reigns of William and Anne, and were, like the penal laws against the Catholics of those reigns, palpable violations of the treaty of Limerick.—Though a glimmering of toleration had found its way into the councils of England, and given rise to "*an act for exempting Protestant dissenters of this country (Ireland) from certain penalties to which they were subject*," the Catholics were excluded, by a particular clause, from any benefit of it. And though it was in this reign that the first act* passed "*for discharging all persons in offices and employments from all penalties which they had incurred by not qualifying themselves, pursuant to an act to prevent the further growth of Popery*," the favour conferred by it was wholly to the Protestant dissenters, as no Catholic had been placed in any public office since the passing of that penal law.

The loyalty of the Catholics was in this reign put to a complete trial by the Scotch rebellion of 1715. If, after having fought three campaigns in

* 6th Geo. I.

in ſupport of James's pretenſions to the throne of Ireland; after having experienced the infraction of every part of the treaty of Limerick, and been expoſed to a code of ſtatutes, by which they were totally excluded from the privileges of the conſtitution; and if, after they had become ſubject "to the worſt of all oppreſſions, the perſecution of private ſociety and private manners,"* they had embarked in the cauſe of the invader, their conduct would have been that of a high ſpirited nation, goaded into a ſtate of deſperation by their relentleſs tormentors, and if their reſiſtance had been ſucceſsful, their leaders would have ranked among the Tell's and Waſhington's of modern hiſtory. But ſo far from yielding to the natural dictates of revenge, or attempting to take advantage of what was paſſing in Scotland to regain their rights, they did not follow the example of their rulers, in violating, upon the firſt favourable opportunity, a ſacred and ſolemn compact; and thus they gave the ſtrongeſt teſtimony, that they had wholly given up their former hopes of eſtabliſhing a Catholic prince

upon

* Burke's Letter to a Peer of Ireland.

upon the throne. Their loyalty was not however a protection to them against the oppressions of their Protestant countrymen. The penalties for the exercise of their religion, were generally and rigidly inflicted. Their chapels were shut up, their priests dragged from their hiding-places, hurried into prisons, and from thence sent into banishment.

GEORGE II.

In this reign, the following additional difabilities were impofed upon the Catholics.

By the 1ft G.II. c.9. fect.7. no Papift could vote at an election without taking the oath of fupremacy. However great the oppreffion which the Catholics had experienced during former reigns, this meafure altogether completed their entire exclufion from the benefits of the Conftitution, and from the opportunity of regaining their former juft rights. It was becaufe this privilege had began to operate amongft Proteftants in a manner very favourable to the Catholics, and to bring about a feeling of regret for their fufferings, and a coalition between the two parties to oppofe the influence of the Englifh Government as a common caufe of grievances, that Primate Boulter advifed the Minifters to pafs this law. His principle of Government for Ireland was to uphold the Englifh intereft by the divifions of the inhabitants; and, on this occafion, it induced him to adopt the defperate refolution

of

of disfranchising, at one stroke, above five-sixths of its population.*

By the first clause of 1st Geo. II. c. 30. barristers, six clerks, &c. are required to take the oath of supremacy.

By the second clause all converts, &c. are bound to educate their children as Protestants.

By 7th Geo. II. c. 5. sect. 12. barristers or solicitors, marrying Papists, are deemed Papists, and made subject to all penalties as such.

By 7th Geo. II. c. 6. no convert can act as a justice of the peace, whose wife or children, under 16 years of age, are educated Papists.

The 13th Geo. II. c. 6. is an act to amend former acts for disarming Papists.

By the 6th clause of this act, Protestants educating their children Papists are made subject to the same disabilities as Papists are.

* Primate Boulter, in his Letter of this year to the Archbishop of Canterbury, (1st vol. p. 210.) says, "There are probably in this kingdom five Papists at least to one Protestant."

By 9th Geo. II. c. 3. no perſon can ſerve on a petty jury, unleſs ſeized of a freehold of 5l. per annum, or, being a Proteſtant, ſhall not be poſſeſſed of a profit rent of 15l. per annum, under a leaſe for years.

By 9th Geo. II. c. 6. ſect. 5. perſons robbed by privateers during war with a Popiſh prince, ſhall be reimburſed by grand jury preſentment, and the money be levied upon the goods and lands of Popiſh inhabitants only.

The 19th Geo. II. c. 5. is an act for granting a duty on hawkers and pedlars to the ſociety of Proteſtant charter-ſchools.

The 19th Geo. II. c. 13. is an act to annul all marriages between Proteſtants and Papiſts, or celebrated by Popiſh prieſts.

By the 23d Geo. II. c. 10. ſect. 3. every Popiſh prieſt who ſhall celebrate any marriage contrary to 12th Geo. I. c. 3. and be thereof convicted, ſhall be hanged.

Of

Of thefe laft acts, and of Lord Chefterfield's administration, Mr. Burke gives the following account. "This man, while he was duping the "credulity of the Papifts with fine words in private, "and commending their good behaviour during a "rebellion in Great Britain, as it well deferved to "be commended and rewarded, was capable of "urging penal laws againft them in a fpeech from "the throne,* and of ftimulating with provocatives "the wearied and half exhaufted bigotry of the "Parliament of Ireland. They fet to work, but "they were at a lofs what to do; for they had "already almoft gone through every contrivance "which could wafte the vigour of their country: "but, after much ftruggle, they produced a child "of their old age, the fhocking and unnatural "act about marriages, which tended to finifh the "fcheme

* "The meafures that have hitherto been taken to prevent the growth of Popery, have, I hope, had fome, and will ftill have a greater effect; however I leave it to your confideration whether nothing further can be done, either by new laws, or by more effectual execution of thofe in being, to fecure the nation againft the greater number of Papifts, whofe fpeculative errors would only deferve pity, if their pernicious influence upon civil fociety did not both require and authorife reftraint." —*Speech to both Houfes of Parliament, October* 8, 1745.— Com. Jour. 7. 642.

" ſcheme for making the people not only two
" diſtinct parties for ever, but keeping them as
" two diſtinct ſpecies in the ſame land. Mr.
" Gardiner's humanity was ſhocked at it, as one
" of the worſt parts of that truly barbarous
" ſyſtem, if one could well ſettle the preference,
" where almoſt all the parts were outrages on
" the rights of humanity and the laws of
" nations."*

Of the conduct of the Catholics during the Scotch rebellion of 1745, fortunately for them, but greatly to the ſhame of thoſe who accuſe them of being actuated by religious principles inconſiſtent with their duty to their ſovereign, there is on record an irrefutable document. In the year 1762, upon a debate in the Houſe of Lords, about the expediency of raiſing five regiments of Catholics for the King of Portugal, the Primate, Dr. Stone, in anſwer to the uſual objections that were urged on all occaſions againſt the good faith and loyalty of that body, declared in his place, " that in the year " 1747, after that rebellion was entirely ſup-" preſſed,

* Letter to a Peer in Ireland.

"pressed, happening to be in England, he had "an opportunity of perusing all the papers of the "rebels, and their correspondents, which were "seized in the custody of Murray, the Pretender's secretary; and that, after having spent "much time, and taken great pains in examining "them, not without some share of the then "common suspicion, that there might be some "private understanding and intercourse between "them and the Irish Catholics, he could not "discover the least trace, hint, or intimation of "such intercourse or correspondence in them, or "of any of the latter's favouring or abetting, or "having been so much as made acquainted with "the designs or proceedings of these rebels. And "what," he said, "he wondered at most of all "was, that in all his researches, he had not met "with any passage in any of these papers, from "which he could infer, that either their Holy "Father, the Pope, or any of his Cardinals, "Bishops, or other Dignitaries of that Church, "or any of the Irish clergy, had either directly, "or indirectly, encouraged, aided, or approved "of the commencing or carrying on of that "rebellion."*

Those

* Curry, Rev. 2. 260.

Thofe of the clergy of England, who lately took fo active a part in exciting and upholding the infamous outcry of "No Popery"—will do well to compare this declaration of Primate Stone, with the following ftatement of the conduct of the Irifh clergy, immediately upon the breaking out of the Scotch rebellion. They will learn how eafily it is, even for the grave profeffion of the church to commit errors, and to pollute its facred character, by embarking in the controverfy of party politics. "The Bifhops wrote paftoral letters to their refpective diocefans to excite the members of the eftablifhed church to enforce all the penal ftatutes, and with equal wifdom and charity, and a ready obedience did the clergy follow the example and directions of their fuperiors, and apply the whole power of their body to fupport the fanatic politics of the day. In their inflammatory fermons they excited religious animofity by reviving the moft fhocking circumftances of the Irifh rebellion of 1641, and of the gun-powder plot in England in 1605. Thefe tranfactions were ftudioufly aggravated, and the crimes, whether real or fuppofed, committed by Catholics, dead more than a century before, was imputed

imputed to all thofe who furvived of the fame religious perfuafion.

If the conduct of the bifhops and clergy was improper, on account of its inconfiftency with thofe principles of univerfal charity, that the gofpel, whofe well paid minifters they were, inculcated; it was ftill more fo in confequence of the total want of grounds, even of fufpicion, that the Catholics were difloyal. Befides, it was indecent in the laft degree for thofe, who were endowed by the ftate for the purpofe only of difcharging the functions of a religious profeffion, to degrade their facred character by affuming the duties of the civil magiftrates, and embarking in all the tumult and paffion of political perfecution. The conduct of the Catholic priefts at this period forms a contraft, by no means creditable to thofe who teach the fuperior tolerance of the Proteftant religion, and ground their animofitities againft the Catholics on the fuppofed illiberality which controuls their principles. This oppreffed and indigent body of men, inftead of taking offence at the proceedings of the bifhops and clergy of the eftablifhed church, "co-operated "with their Proteſtant brethren, to maintain "order and tranquility. Their paſtoral letters, "public diſcourſes from the pulpit, and private "admonitions, were equally directed for the ſer- "vice of the government."* Yet theſe clergy were the members of that church, the principles of which are ſtated to be of ſuch a nature by many of the Engliſh clergy, as to render it abſolutely impoſſible, that a Catholic can be a good ſubject; an opinion, however, which muſt vaniſh, before this and other equally ſtrong proofs, of the uniform and deeply rooted loyalty of the Iriſh Catholics.

On the 26th September, 1757, the Duke of Bedford was ſworn in Lord Lieutenant. His open declarations of liberal ſentiments towards the Catholics, and ſome communications that were made for the firſt time ſince the paſſing of the ferocious act of Anne, to pervert the growth of Popery, of an intention to repeal ſome part of the penal laws, encouraged them to hope for a change in the ſyſtem of Iriſh government. Ten days after

* Cheſterfield's Works, 1. 150. Ir. Ed.

after his arrival, the Catholic clergy of Dublin, influenced by thefe communications, read the following exhortation to their refpective congregations. This exhortation forms the firft and a very important document in proof of the fufferings, the refignation, and the loyalty of the Catholic body. It is one peculiarly deferving of the attention, as being well calculated to remove the ignorance and prejudices of thofe who ftill perfift in calumniating the Catholic clergy of Ireland as enemies to the King and Conftitution.

Exhortation of the Roman Catholic Clergy of Dublin, read from their Altars on the 2d of October, 1757.

It is now time, Chriftians, that you return your moft grateful thanks to the Almighty God, who, after vifiting you with a fcarcity, which approached near unto a famine, has been gracioufly pleafed, like a merciful father, to hear your prayers, and feed you with a plentiful harveft; nor ought you to forget thofe kind benefactors, who, in the fevereft times, mindful only of the public good, generoufly beftowed, without any diftinction of perfons, thofe large charities, by which thoufands were preferved, who otherwife muft have perifhed the victims of hunger and poverty. We ought efpecially to be moft earneft in our thanks to the chief governors and magiftrates of the kingdom, and of this city in particular, who, on this occafion, proved the fathers and faviours of the nation. But as we have not a more effectual method of fhewing our acknowledgment to our temporal governors, than by an humble, peaceful, and obedient behaviour; as hitherto, we earnestly exhort you to continue in the same happy and Christian disposition, and thus, by degrees, you will entirely efface in their minds those evil impressions, which have been conceived so much to our prejudice, and industriously propagated by our enemies. A series of more than sixty years spent, with a pious resignation, under the hardships of very severe penal laws, and with the greatest thankfulness for the lenity and moderation, with which they were executed, ever since the accession of the present royal family, is certainly a fact which must outweigh, in the minds of all unbiassed persons, any misconceived opinions of the doctrine and tenets of our holy church.

You know that it has always been our constant practice, as ministers of Jesus Christ, to inspire you with the greatest horror for thefts, frauds, murders, and the like abominable crimes; as being contrary to the laws of God and nature, destructive of civil society, condemned by our most holy church, which, so far from justifying them on the score of religion, or any other pretext whatsoever, delivers the unrepenting authors of such criminal practices over to Satan.

We are no less zealous than ever in exhorting you to abstain from cursing, swearing, and blaspheming; detestable vices, to which the poorer sort of our people are most unhappily addicted, and which must at one time or other bring down the vengeance of heaven upon you in some visible punishment, unless you absolutely refrain from them.

It is probable, that, from hence, some people have taken occasion to brand us with this infamous calumny, that we need not fear to take false oaths, and consequently to perjure ourselves; as if we believed that any power upon earth could

authorise

authorise such damnable practices, or grant dispensations for this purpose. How unjust and cruel this charge is, you know by our instructions to you both in public and private, in which we have ever condemned such doctrines, as false and impious. Others, likewise, may easily know it from the constant behaviour of numbers of Roman Catholics, who have given the strongest proofs of their abhorrence of those tenets, by refusing to take oaths, which, however conducive to their temporal interest, appeared to them entirely repugnant to the principles of their religion.

We must now intreat you, dear Christians, to offer up your most fervent prayers to the Almighty God, who holds in his hands the hearts of kings and princes, beseech him to direct the counsels of our rulers, to inspire them with sentiments of moderation and compassion towards us. We ought to be more earnest, at this juncture, in our supplications to heaven; *as some very honourable personages have encouraged us to hope for a mitigation of the penal laws.* Pray then the Almighty to give a blessing to these their generous designs, and to aid their counsels, in such a manner, that, whilst they intend to assist us, like kind benefactors, they may not, contrary to their intentions, by mistaking the means, most irretrievably destroy us.

To conclude, be just in your dealings, sober in your conduct, religious in your practice, avoid riots, quarrels, and tumults; and thus you will approve yourselves good citizens, peaceable subjects, and pious Christians.

Instead, however, of a repeal taking place of any of the penal laws, rumours began very generally

rally

rally to prevail, of its being the intention of government to proceed to carry into effect a bill, that had been prepared by the former administration, for altering the law respecting the registry of the clergy. The existing law, which passed in the reign of Queen Anne, had been found too penal to admit of its being carried into execution; and thus, by an excess of tyranny, was the object of it wholly defeated. In the place of this law, it had been proposed to pass one with such provisions, that it should, like the other penal laws, execute itself; and, upon this project being now revived, the Catholics, for the first time since 1704, took measures as a body to vindicate their religious and civil principles. Mr. Charles O'Connor, the celebrated Irish scholar and antiquarian, with the assistance of Dr. Curry, the author of the Review of the Civil Wars of Ireland, and Mr. Wyse, of Waterford, exerted themselves with good effect in persuading their suffering countrymen of the necessity of coming forward to induce their rulers to admit them into a participation of the privileges of the constitution. As a ground-work of their future labour, Dr. O'Keefe, the titular Bishop of Kildare, proposed, at a meeting

ing held at Lord Trimlefton's, a declaration of the principles of their church, as far as they could bear upon their civil duties, to be figned by the chiefs of their body, and publifhed as an anfwer to the mifreprefentations and calumnies they had laboured under fince the reformation of the national religion: this declaration was unanimoufly adopted; it was figned by many clergymen and gentlemen of rank and property, and fent to Rome, as the act and deed of the Irifh Catholics. It is as follows:*

Whereas certain opinions and principles, inimical to good order and government, have been attributed to the Catholics, the exiftence of which we utterly deny; and whereas it is at this time peculiarly neceffary to remove fuch imputations, and to give the moft full and ample fatisfaction to our Proteftant brethren, that we hold no principle whatfoever incompatible with our duty as men or as fubjects, or repugnant to liberty, whether political, civil, or religious.

Now we, the Catholics of Ireland, for the removal of all fuch imputations, and in deference to the opinion of many refpectable bodies of men, and individuals among our Proteftant brethren, do hereby, in the face of our country, of all Europe, and before God, make this our deliberate and folemn declaration:

1ft.

* This declaration was republifhed in 1792.—*Plowden, v.* 3. *p.* 179.

1st. We abjure, disavow, and condemn the opinion, that princes, excommunicated by the pope and council, *or by any ecclesiastical authority whatsoever*, may therefore be deposed or murdered by their subjects, or any other persons. We hold such doctrine in detestation, as wicked and impious; and we declare that we do not believe, that either the pope, with or without a general council, or *any prelate or priest, or any ecclesiastical power whatsoever*, can absolve the subjects of this kingdom, or any of them, from their allegiance to his Majesty King George the Third, who is, by authority of Parliament, the lawful king of this realm.

2d. We abjure, condemn, and detest, as unchristian and impious, the principle, that it is lawful to murder, destroy, or any ways injure any person whatsoever, for or under the pretence of being heretics; and we declare solemnly before God, that we believe that *no act, in itself unjust, immoral, or wicked, can ever be justified or excused by, or under pretence or colour, that it was done either for the good of the church, or in obedience to any ecclesiastical power whatsoever.*

3d. We further declare, that we hold it as an unchristian and impious principle, that "no faith is to be kept with heretics." This doctrine we detest and reprobate, not only as *contrary* to our religion, but as destructive of morality, of society, and even of common honesty; and it is our firm belief, that an oath made to *any* person, not of the Catholic religion, is equally binding, as if it were made to any Catholic whatsoever.

4th. We have been charged with holding as an article of our belief, that the pope, with or without the authority of a general council, or that certain ecclesiastical powers can acquit and absolve us, before God, from our oath of allegiance, or

even

even from the juſt oaths and contracts entered into between man and man.

Now we do utterly renounce, abjure, and deny, that we hold or maintain any ſuch belief, as being contrary to the peace and happineſs of ſociety, inconſiſtent with morality, and above all, *repugnant to the true ſpirit of the Catholic religion.*

5th. We do further declare, that we do not believe that the pope of Rome, or any other prince, prelate, ſtate, or potentate, hath, or ought to have, any temporal or civil juriſdiction, power, ſuperiority, or pre-eminence, directly or indirectly, within this realm.

6th. After what we have renounced, it is immaterial, in a political light, what may be our opinion or faith in other points reſpecting the Pope: however, for greater ſatisfaction we declare, that it is *not* an article of the Catholic faith, neither are we thereby required to believe or profeſs, "that the Pope is infallible," or that we are bound to obey any order, in its own nature immoral, though the Pope, or any eccleſiaſtical power, ſhould iſſue or direct ſuch order; but, *on the contrary*, we hold, that it would be *ſinful* in us to pay any reſpect or obedience thereto.

7th. We further declare, that we do not believe that any ſin whatſoever committed by us can be forgiven at the mere will of any Pope, or of any prieſt, or of any perſon or perſons whatſoever; but, that *ſincere ſorrow for paſt ſins*, a firm and ſincere reſolution, as far as may be in our power, to reſtore our neighbour's property or character, if we have treſpaſſed on, or unjuſtly injured either; *a firm and ſincere reſolution to avoid future guilt*, and to atone to God, are *previous and indiſpenſable* requiſites to eſtabliſh a well-founded expectation of forgiveneſs; and that any perſon who receives abſolution

 without

without theſe previous requiſites, ſo far from obtaining thereby any remiſſion of his ſins, incurs the additional guilt of violating a ſacrament.

8th. We do hereby ſolemnly diſclaim, and for ever renounce all intereſt in, and title to all forfeited lands, reſulting from any rights, or ſuppoſed rights, of our anceſtors, or any claim, title, or intereſt therein; nor do we admit any title, as a foundation of right, which is *not eſtabliſhed and acknowledged by the laws of the realm, as they now ſtand.* We deſire further, that whenever the patriotiſm, liberality, and juſtice of our countrymen, ſhall reſtore to us a participation in the elective franchiſe, no Catholic ſhall be permitted to vote at any election for members to ſerve in parliament, until he ſhall previouſly take an oath *to defend, to the utmoſt of his power,* the arrangement of property in this country, *as eſtabliſhed by the different acts of attainder and ſettlement.*

9th. It has been objected to us, that we wiſh to ſubvert the preſent church eſtabliſhment, for the purpoſe of ſubſtituting a Catholic eſtabliſhment in its ſtead: Now we do hereby diſclaim, diſavow, and ſolemnly abjure any ſuch intention; and further, if we ſhall be admitted into any ſhare of the conſtitution, by our being reſtored to the right of elective franchiſe, we are ready, in the moſt ſolemn manner, to declare, that we will not exerciſe that privilege to diſturb and weaken the eſtabliſhment of the Proteſtant religion, or Proteſtant government in this country.

Though this declaration did not produce any change of conduct on the part of the Engliſh government at that time, its failure can only be attributed to the obſtinacy with which the principle of of governing Ireland, upon the ſyſtem of ſeparate intereſts between the Proteſtants and Catholics, was adhered to. That ſyſtem is now happily expoſed; and though of late attempted to be revived by his Majeſty's preſent Miniſters, the intelligence and liberality of the preſent race of Iriſh Proteſtants has completely counteracted their factious deſigns. This declaration, though at firſt ineffectual, has, and muſt continue to open the eyes of mankind to the true character of the Iriſh Catholic, and to ſecure to them the reward which it deſerves, the unlimited confidence of their King and fellow-ſubjects, and the entire reſtoration of their conſtitutional rights. The ſentiments contained in it are thoſe of true and ſound Chriſtianity, benevolence, and humanity. It is impoſſible that any perſon capable of breathing them can be a bad Chriſtian, a bad ſubject, or a bad man.

In the year 1759, when it was known that a French force, under the command of Conflans, was collected to invade Ireland, the conduct of the Catholics on this, as it had uniformly been on ſimilar occaſions, was loyal in the extreme. Mr. O'Connor, Dr. Curry, and Mr. Wyſe had ſometime before, in 1757, ſucceeded in eſtabliſhing a general committee of the Catholic body, formed by delegates of pariſhes and the principal Catholic nobility and gentry. As ſoon as this invaſion was announced to parliament by a meſſage from the Duke of Bedford, this committee was ſummoned to meet; and Mr. O'Connor having ſubmitted to it the following addreſs to the Lord Lieutenant, it was unanimouſly approved of.

May it pleaſe your Grace,

We, his Majeſty's dutiful and faithful ſubjects, the Roman Catholic gentlemen, merchants, and citizens of Dublin, do, with the greateſt reſpect, approach the illuſtrious repreſentative of the beſt of Kings, with our hearty congratulations on thoſe glorious ſucceſſes, by ſea and land, which have attended his Majeſty's arms, in the proſecution of this juſt and neceſſary war.

We gratefully acknowledge the lenity extended to us by his moſt ſacred Majeſty, and by his royal father, of happy memory. Our allegiance, may it pleaſe your Grace, is confirmed by affection and gratitude; our religion commands it; and it ſhall be our invariable rule firmly and inviolably to adhere to it.

We are called to this duty, at the preſent time in particular, when a foreign enemy is meditating deſperate attempts to interrupt

terrupt the happineſs and diſturb the repoſe, which theſe kingdoms have ſo long enjoyed, under a Monarch, who places his chief glory in proving himſelf the common father of all his people: and we ſincerely aſſure your Grace, that we are ready and willing, to the utmoſt of our abilities, to aſſiſt in ſupporting his Majeſty's government againſt all hoſtile attempts whatſoever.

Whenever, my Lord, it ſhall pleaſe the Almighty, that the legiſlative power of this realm ſhall deem the peaceable conduct of his Majeſty's Catholic ſubjects of Ireland, for many years paſt, an object worthy of its favourable attention, we humbly hope means may then be deviſed, to render ſo numerous a body more uſeful members to the community, and more ſtrengthening friends to the ſtate, than they could poſſibly have hitherto been, under the reſtraint of the many penal laws againſt them. We moſt humbly beſeech your Grace to repreſent to his Majeſty theſe ſentiments and reſolutions of his Majeſty's faithful ſubjects, the Roman Catholics of this metropolis, who ſincerely wiſh, that a peace honourable to his Majeſty, and advantageous to his kingdoms, may be the iſſue of the preſent war; and that the people of Ireland may be long governed by your Grace, a Viceroy, in whom wiſdom, moderation, and juſtice, are ſo eminently conſpicuous.

On that occaſion, alſo, the wealthy individuals of this perſuaſion offered to accommodate the government with large ſums of money, in caſe of neceſſity, to ſupport the Proteſtant eſtabliſhment againſt all its enemies; and the Catholics

Catholics of the city of Cork, in a body, presented an addrefs to the Lord Lieutenant, expreffing their loyalty in the warmeft terms of affurance. They profeffed the warmeft indignation at the threatened invafion of the kingdom, by an enemy vainly flattered with the imaginary hope of affiftance in Ireland, from the former attachments of their deluded predeceffors. They affured his Grace that fuch fchemes were altogether inconfiftent with their principles and intentions; and that they would, to the utmoft exertion of their abilities, with their lives and fortunes, join in the defence and fupport of his Majefty's royal perfon and government, againft all invaders whatfoever.*

Thefe circumftances are proofs of no ordinary fidelity in the Irifh Catholics to the Houfe of Brunfwick. They were, however, of no avail in mitigating the rigour of the magiftracy in the execution of the penal laws, or in inducing the Britifh government to repeal any part of them; for the reign of George II. clofed without any grateful acknowledgment being

made

* Smollet's Hiftory of England, 4. 69.

made to them for the ſteadineſs with which they reſiſted the temptation that was held out to them in 1745 and 1759 to ſupport the claims of a Catholic pretender to the throne of Great Britain.

GEORGE III.

Notwithſtanding the firſt meaſure of this reign, the royal recommendation to Parliament to make the judges independent of the Crown, beſpoke the determination of his Majeſty to reſpect the feelings and confirm the rights and liberties of his ſubjects; ſtill the unfortunate Catholics of Ireland were doomed to ſuffer under new pains and penalties.

In the year 1776, an act of Parliament was paſſed,* by which one or more juſtices of the peace, and all ſheriffs and chief magiſtrates of cities and towns corporate, within their reſpective juriſdictions, may from time to time, as well by night as by day, ſearch for and ſeize all arms and ammunition belonging to any Papiſt not entitled to keep the ſame, or in the hands of any perſon in truſt, for a Papiſt; and for that purpoſe enter any dwelling-houſe, out-houſe, office, field

* 15th and 16th Geo. III. c. 21. § 15.

field or other place belonging to a Papiſt, or to any other perſon where ſuch magiſtrate has reaſonable cauſe to *ſuſpect* any ſuch arms or ammunition ſhall be concealed; and *on ſuſpicion*, after ſearch, may ſummon and examine on oath, the perſon *ſuſpected* of ſuch concealment.

By the 17th clauſe of this act, Papiſts refuſing to deliver up or declare ſuch arms as they, or any with their privity, have, or hindering the delivery, or refuſing to diſcover on oath, or without cauſe neglecting to appear on ſummons to be examined before a magiſtrate concerning the ſame, ſhall, on conviction, be puniſhed by fine and impriſonment, or *ſuch corporeal puniſhment of pillory or whipping*, as the Court ſhall in their diſcretion think proper.

In the year 1782, a clauſe was introduced into an act,* by which no perſon ſhall be admitted into the Society of King's Inns as a ſtudent, who ſhall not, at the time of his admiſſion, be a Proteſtant.

* 21st and 22d Geo. III. c. 32. § 2.

In the ſame year, an act* was paſſed, by the 3d clauſe of which, all ſtatutes made in England or Great Britain, and all ſuch clauſes and proviviſions contained in any ſtatute there made, as relate to the taking any oath or oaths, or making or ſubſcribing any declaration in Ireland, or to any penalty or diſability for omitting the ſame, ſhall be accepted, uſed, and executed in Ireland.

This act referred to: 1ſt, the Engliſh act of 3d William and Mary, c. 2. ſect. 1, 4, 5, 6, 7, by which the oath of ſupremacy mentioned in 2. Eliz. 1. c. 1. is abrogated, and a new oath of ſupremacy is required to be taken by all perſons admitted in Ireland to hold any civil or military office, and by members of both Houſes of Parliament; 2dly, to the Engliſh act of 1ſt Anne, ſtat. 2. c. 17. requiring all perſons to take the oath of abjuration, preſcribed by the Engliſh acts of 13th Wm. III. c. 6. and 1ſt Anne, ſt. 1. c. 22d; 3dly, to the Engliſh act of 6th Geo. III. c. 53. § 2. declaring that from the 1ſt Auguſt, 1776, the oath of abjuration, by this act appointed to be taken

* 21st and 22d Geo. III. c. 48. § 3.

taken in Great Britain, ſhall be the oath of abjuration, to be taken in Ireland.

Though this clauſe of the 21ſt and 22d of Geo. III. c. 48. has attracted very little public attention, it was of no leſs import than that of being the firſt legal excluſion of Catholics from ſitting in the Iriſh Parliament. They had been excluded *de facto* by their voluntary ſubmiſſion to the Engliſh act of 3d William and Mary, but not *de jure* till this act of 21ſt and 22d Geo. III. rendered the act of William and Mary, binding in Ireland.

This circumſtance, which has always been overlooked, even by the Catholics themſelves, proves how readily they have been inclined at all times to ſubmit to the authority of Government. And it alſo proves how unfounded thoſe arguments are, which maintain that the excluſion of the Catholics of Ireland from Parliament, is a principle on which the family of his Majeſty was placed upon the throne. It completely overturns the ſyſtem of erroneous reaſoning concerning the coronation oath, which of late has been ſo common; and, ſo far as the meaning of this oath is at iſſue, it reduces the queſtion to this ſimple point, whether the King can conſcientiouſly place the Catholics of Ireland in the ſame condition, with reſpect to ſitting in Parliament, in which they had continued till the twenty-ſecond year of his own reign.

In 1785 an act was paſſed * for granting 4000l. to be expended in apprentice fees, to ſuch tradeſmen or manufacturers, as ſhould take children from charter-ſchools or the Foundling Hoſpital; but it was expreſsly provided that the children ſhould be bound to none but Proteſtant tradeſmen and manufacturers.

The whole code of the penal ſtatutes againſt the Catholics of Ireland is now laid before the view of the reader, under which they ſo long and ſo patiently languiſhed; ſtatutes unexampled for their inhumanity, their unwarrantableneſs and their impolicy, which were adopted to exterminate a race of men already cruſhed and broken by the longeſt ſeries of calamities which one nation had

* 25th of George III. c. 48. § 11 and 12.

had ever the opportunity of inflicting upon another. They were framed againſt Chriſtians under the pretence of ſecuring religion ; they were the work of Proteſtants, than whom no ſect has cried out more loudly againſt perſecution when Proteſtants were the martyrs. They were ſanctioned by a nation who owed its liberties, and by monarchs who owed their throne, to a ſolemn covenant that they ſhould never exiſt. Here may we not inquire, if the Engliſh nation, legiſlature, and King, have not a duty to fulfil towards the Iriſh Catholics even greater than that of juſtice—a duty of compunction, of repentance, and atonement? The faith of a ſolemn treaty made with them has been broken: it is not enough that it has been in part re-eſtabliſhed, it ought to be religiouſly fulfilled. They have been ruled with tyranny: it is not enough that the tyranny ſhould be relaxed, it ſhould ceaſe altogether. They have been driven from the pale of the Conſtitution: it is not enough that they ſhould be allowed to paſs its barriers, they ſhould range free and uncontrouled through all its rights.

That

That this ſyſtem of ſlow political torture, was not warranted by any alleged delinquency on their part is notorious, for it was deviſed and perfected in times of profound tranquility. That they were not deſerving even of the ſuſpicion of being diſloyal ſubjects, is proved by their ſignal forbearance, which has preſerved the empire from the calamitous conſequences of ſuch flagitious miſgovernment; and that, on the contrary, they fully merited the confidence and protection of the legiſlature, no fair and candid mind can deny, when it gives to their conduct, in ſtrictly adhering to the ſtipulations of the treaty of Limerick, and to their allegiance to the Houſe of Brunſwick, the juſt value to which it is entitled.

Having now reached the utmoſt point to which the penal ſtatutes extended, which ſeems to be as far as human invention, quickened by mixed feelings of alarm, of bigotry and of pride, could go, we ſhould deprive political ſcience of a great ſource of concluſive demonſtration, if we neglected to record its effects.

But there is even a nearear intereſt in this examination. At a period when the ſtate of Ireland ſo much occupies the attention of the Legiſlature and of the public; when it is admitted on all ſides, that the proſperity and ſecurity of England herſelf muſt riſe or fall with the proſperity and ſecurity of Ireland; and when the events of each ſucceeding day prove the abſolute neceſſity of ſome meaſures to ameliorate her condition, and that things cannot go on, as they are, without the inevitable deſtruction of the Britiſh empire; it will be of great importance to be able to form an accurate opinion upon the effects which were the reſult of the penal ſtatutes. If it can be proved that the paſt and preſent ſtate of diſcontent and poverty, which has been, and ſtill is, the characteriſtic of Ireland, is the natural conſequence of theſe laws, then no man can diſpute the policy of ſeeking the remedy of it by the total repeal of them. If, on the other hand, no ſuch proof can be brought forward, and it ſhall appear that theſe laws are not the origin of Iriſh diſcontent and poverty, then indeed it will be the duty of every one to accede to the doctrines of thoſe more able ſtateſmen, who

ſolve

ſolve the difficulty, by ſuppoſing, what has been aſſerted of the negro race, that the Iriſh are an inferior, ſemibrutal people, ſubmitted, by the neceſſity of nature, to a ſtate of ſlavery, and unfit to be admitted to the privileges of Engliſhmen.

It appears from unqueſtionable authority, that, during the interval that elapſed between the ſurrender of Limerick, and the total infraction of the treaty in 1704, by the act to prevent the further growth of Popery, the toleration which the Catholics experienced by virtue of that treaty, produced its natural conſequences. The ſecurity they enjoyed, reſtored induſtry and plenty of all things: uſeful arts were introduced; the land cultivated; and a fine iſland, reduced to a deſert by the late war, ſoon aſſumed a new face. In fact, Ireland was never happier than during this interval of religious toleration.* Of the effects of the penal laws in entirely reverſing this order of things, Lord Taffe, in his valuable tract on Iriſh Affairs, gives the following deſcription. "Thoſe penalties and interdicts (by the laws of "Anne) had their natural effects in the diſpeo-

"pling

* Obſervations on the Affairs of Ireland, by Lord Taaffe, p. 4.

" pling greatly the three fine provinces, wherein " the bulk of Catholics reside. They took their " effect in putting a stop to the cultivation began " in King William's reign. No sooner were the " Catholics excluded from durable and profitable " tenures, than they commenced graziers, and " laid aside agriculture: they ceased from drain- " ing and enclosing their farms, and building " good houses, as occupations unsuited to the " new part assigned them in our national economy. " They fell to wasting the lands they were vir- " tually forbid to cultivate, the business of pas- " turage being compatible with such a conduct, " and requiring also little industry and less labour " in the management."*

In the year 1723, the wretchedness of the people of Ireland was so great, that the Duke of Grafton, in a speech from the throne, recommended parliament to take measures for relieving them. The distress, however, continued; and in a petition presented to the House of Commons, in the same year, by the woollen manufacturers, they say, " The woollen manufacture of this

* Ibid. p. 11.

" kingdom, which is confined to our own con-
" ſumption, has of late been ſo conſiderably leſſen-
" ed, that ſeveral thouſand families have been for-
" ced to beg alms and charity of good chriſtians;
" and that a collection had lately been made
" throughout the whole city to relieve them."*

Primate Boulter, in a letter of the 25th of March, 1722, to the Duke of Newcaſtle, bears teſtimony to this wretched ſtate of Ireland; he ſays, " Since I came here in the year 1725,
" there was almoſt a famine among the poor;
" laſt year the dearneſs of corn was ſuch, that
" thouſands of families quitted their habitations,
" to ſeek bread elſewhere, and many hundreds
" periſhed:"† again on the 23d of November, 1728, he ſays, in writing to the Duke, " I am
" ſorry I am obliged to give your Grace ſo melan-
" choly an account of the ſtate of the kingdom,
" as I ſhall in this letter."

But one of the moſt pernicious effects of theſe penal laws was the emigration of the principal Catholic families to the Continent. They carried with

* Com. Jour. v. 3. p. 24.

† Letters, p. 226.

with them the greater part of thofe qualifications, which render a country civilized, tranquil and profperous; they left the mafs of the Catholic population, without the influence of men of education and property, to direct and controul their conduct; and in the place of fecuring their own country, they filled, with the higheft credit to themfelves, the fituations of ftatefmen and generals, in thofe nations which were hoftile to the interefts of Great Britain.

Of the effect thefe laws had exhibited, in their avowed objects of propagating the Proteftant religion, and promoting the national profperity, it is impoffible to give a more able or a more accurate defcription than the following, by Mr. Arthur Young, who was in Ireland at the period we now treat of:* "While property lay expofed "to the practices of power, the great body of "the people, who had been ftripped of their "all, were more enraged than converted: they "adhered to the perfuafion of their forefathers, "with the fteadieft and moft determined zeal; "while the priefts, actuated by the fpirit of a "thoufand inducements, made profelytes among

 "the

* 1778.

" the common Proteſtants, in defiance of every " danger. And the great glaring fact yet " remains, and is even admitted by the warmeſt " advocates for the laws of diſcovering that the " eſtabliſhed religion has not gained upon the " Catholic in point of numbers, but on the " contrary, that the latter has been rather on the " increaſe. Public liſts have been returned from " the ſeveral dioceſes which confirm this fact; " and the intelligence I received on my journey " ſpoke the ſame language.

" As it is the great body of the common " people that forms the ſtrength of a country, " when willing ſubjects, and its weakneſs when " ill-affected, this fact is a deciſion of the queſ- " tion: After 70 years undiſturbed operation, " the ſyſtem adopted in Queen Anne's reign " has failed in this great aim, and meets at this " day with a more numerous and equally de- " termined body of Catholics, than it had to " oppoſe when firſt promulgated. Has not the " experience of every age and every nation, " proved that the effect is invariable and uni- " verſal? Let a religion be what it may, and

" under

" under whatever circumſtances, no ſyſtem of " perſecution ever yet had any other effect, than to " confirm its profeſſors in their tenets, and ſpread " their doctrines, inſtead of reſtraining them. " The great plea of the Roman Catholic prieſts, " and their merit with their congregations, are the " dangers they hazard, and the perſecutions they " ſuffer for the ſake of their faith; arguments " that had and ever will have weight, while " human nature continues formed of its preſent " materials.

" But if theſe exertions of a ſucceſſion of " ignorant legiſlatures have failed continually " in propagating the religion of government, " much more have they failed in the great " object of natural proſperity. The only con- " ſiderable manufacture in Ireland, which carries " in all parties the appearance of induſtry, is " the linen, and it ought never be forgotten " that this is ſolely confined to the Proteſtant " parts of the kingdom. The poor Catholics " in the ſouth of Ireland ſpin wool generally, " but the purchaſers of their labour, and the " whole worſted trade, is in the hands of the

" Quakers of Clonmel, Carrick and Bandon, &c. " The fact is, the professors of that religion " are under such discouragements, that they can- " not engage in any trade which requires both " industry and capital. If they succeed and " make a fortune, what are they to do with it? " They can neither buy land, nor take a mort- " gage, nor even fine down the rent of a lease, " Where is there a people in the world to be " found industrious under such circumstances?

" It is no superficial view I have taken of this " matter in Ireland; and being at Dublin at the " time a very trifling part of these laws was " agitated in parliament, I attended the debates, " with my mind open to conviction, and an " auditor for the mere purposes of information. " I have conversed on the subject with most dis- " tinguished characters of the kingdom, and I " cannot after all but declare that the scope, pur- " port, and aim of the laws of discovery, as " executed, are not against the Catholic religion, " which increases under them, but against the " industry and property of whosoever professes " that religion. In vain has it been said, that

" consequence

" consequence and power follow property, and " that the attack is made in order to wound the " doctrine through its property. If such was the " intention, I reply, that seventy years expe- " rience prove the folly and futility of it. Those " laws have crushed all the industry, and " wrested most of the property from the " Catholics; but the religion triumphs; it is " thought to increase. Those who have handed " about calculations to prove a decrease, admit " on the face of them, that it will require " 4000 YEARS to make converts of the whole, " supposing the work to go on in future, as it " has in the past time. But the whole pretence " is an affront to common sense, for it implies, " that you will lessen a religion, by persecuting " it: all history and experience condemn such a " proposition.

" The system pursued in Ireland has had no " other tendency but that of driving out of " the kingdom all the personal wealth of the " Catholics, and prohibiting their industry within " it. The face of the country, every object, " in short, which presents itself to the eye of a

" traveller,

"traveller, tells him how effectually this has "been done. I urge it not as an argument, "the whole kingdom speaks it as a fact. We "have seen that this conduct has not converted "the people to the religion of government; and "instead of adding to the internal security, it "has endangered it: if therefore it does not add "to the national prosperity, for what purpose, "but that of private tyranny, could it have "been embraced and persisted in? Mistaken "ideas of private interest account for the actions "of individuals; but what could have influenced "the British government to permit a system "which must inevitably prevent the island from "even becoming of the importance which nature "intended?"*

Of the state of the agriculture of Ireland at this period, a tolerable accurate idea may be formed from the words of the same author.— "I have reason to believe that five pounds sterling "per English acre, expended all over Ireland, "which amounts to 88,341,136l. would not more "than build, fence, plant, drain and improve that 'country,

* Young's Tour, vol. 2. 135. Eng. Ed.

"country, to be upon a par in thoſe reſpects with "England."* The prices alſo of the produce of land, afford proof of the general poverty of the kingdom. In 1778, butter ſold for 5¾d. per lb.—mutton, 2¾d.—beef, 2½d.—pork, 2¼d.—veal, 3½d.—a fat turkey for 10¾d.—a gooſe for 8½d.—and a chicken for 2½d.

If further evidence were wanting to eſtabliſh the fact of the penal laws having impoveriſhed Ireland, it is to be found in the following confeſſion of the late Lord Clare. "It was impoſ-"ſible," ſays he, "that any country could conti-"nue to exiſt under a code of laws, by which a "majority of its inhabitants were cut off from the "rights of property. It was a code highly inju-"rious to the landed intereſt of Ireland, and in-"evitably diminiſhed the value of every man's "eſtate, who voted for it."

From theſe ſeveral authorities upon the ſtate of Ireland in 1778, much information may be collected concerning the cauſes of many of thoſe peculiar circumſtances which, at this day, belong to

 that

* Young's Tour, App.

that country. If it is aſked, why the people of Ireland are ſo illiterate? The anſwer that preſents itſelf is, look to the penal laws, that deprived them, till a late period, of education. If it is aſked, why they are poor? The ſame anſwer muſt be given, look to the penal laws. If it is aſked, why the lower orders eat vegetables only, and live in hovels? Still the ſame anſwer, look to the penal laws. If it is aſked, why there is no claſs of yeomanry in Ireland like that in England? The anſwer is, becauſe the penal laws prohibited induſtry, and deprived the former of his property in land as faſt as he could accumulate it. If it is aſked, why the people are diſcontented and diſlike England? This anſwer only can be given, becauſe from England they received this penal code, under which they have endured, for above a century, every ſpecies of calamity, contrary to the poſitive ſtipulations of a ſacred and ſolemn treaty. If, in this era of civilized Europe, Ireland is more backward, its people leſs poliſhed, its wealth leſs extenſive, and its general character below the rank of other countries, it is not now poſſible to miſtake the cauſe. And when all agree that this cauſe is the penal code againſt the Catholics, what

reaſoning

reasoning can contend against the proposition, that all the laws must be repealed in order to remedy the present distempered condition of Ireland?

It was in the year 1774, that the Irish Legislature passed the first act towards conciliating the Catholics, "an act to enable his Majesty's subjects, "of whatever persuasion, to testify their allegiance "to him."* Which is as follows:

Whereas many of his Majesty's subjects in this kingdom are desirous to testify their loyalty and allegiance to his Majesty, and their abhorrence of certain doctrines imputed to them, and to remove jealousies which hereby have for a length of time subsisted between them, and others his Majesty's loyal subjects; but upon account of their religious tenets are, by the laws now in being, prevented from giving public assurances of such allegiance, and of their real principles, and good will, and affection towards their fellow subjects; in order therefore to give such persons an opportunity of testifying their allegiance to his Majesty, and good will towards the present Constitution of this kingdom, and to promote peace and industry amongst the inhabitants thereof, be it enacted by the King's most excellent Majesty, by and with the advice and consent of the Lords Spiritual and Temporal, and Commons in this present Parliament assembled, and by the authority of the same, that from and after the first day of June one thousand seven hundred and seventy-four, it shall and may be lawful for any person professing the Popish religion, to go before the Judges of his Majesty's Court of King's Bench, any justice

* 13th and 14th Geo. III. c. 35.

of the peace for the county in which he does or ſhall reſide, or before any magiſtrate of any city or town corporate wherein he does or ſhall reſide, and there take and ſubſcribe the oath of allegiance and declaration herein after-mentioned; which oath and declaration ſuch judges of the King's Bench, juſtices of the peace, and magiſtrates, are hereby enabled and required to adminiſter;

"I A. B. do take Almighty God, and his only Son Jeſus Chriſt my Redeemer, to witneſs, that I will be faithful and bear true allegiance to our moſt gracious Sovereign Lord King George the Third, and him will defend to the utmoſt of my power againſt all conſpiracies and attempts whatever, that ſhall be made againſt his perſon, crown, and dignity; and I will do my utmoſt endeavour to diſcloſe and make known to his Majeſty, and his heirs, all treaſons and traitorous conſpiracies which may be formed againſt him or them; and I do faithfully promiſe to maintain, ſupport, and defend, to the utmoſt of my power, the ſucceſſion of the Crown in his Majeſty's family, againſt any perſon or perſons whatſoever; hereby utterly renouncing and abjuring any obedience or allegiance unto the perſon taking upon himſelf the ſtile and title of Prince of Wales in the life-time of his father, and who ſince his death is ſaid to have aſſumed the ſtile and title of King of Great Britain and Ireland, by the name of Charles the Third, and to any other perſon claiming or pretending a right to the Crown of theſe realms; and I do ſwear, that I do reject and deteſt, as unchriſtian and impious to believe, that it is lawful to murder or deſtroy any perſon or perſons whatſoever for or under pretence of their being hereticks; and alſo that unchriſtian and impious principle, that no faith is to be kept with hereticks; I further declare, that it is no article of my faith, and that I do renounce, reject, and abjure the opinion, that Princes excommunicated by the Pope and Council, or by any authority of the ſee of Rome, or by any authority

thority whatſoever, may be depoſed and murdered by their ſubjects, or by any perſon whatſoever; and I do promiſe, that I will not hold, maintain, or abet any ſuch opinion, or any other opinion contrary to what is expreſſed in this declaration; and I do declare that I do not believe that the Pope of Rome, or any other foreign Prince, Prelate, State, or Potentate, hath or ought to have any temporal or civil juriſdiction, power, ſuperiority, or pre-eminence, directly or indirectly, within this realm; and I do ſolemnly, in the preſence of God, and of his only Son Jeſus Chriſt my Redeemer, profeſs, teſtify, and declare, that I do make this declaration, and every part thereof, in the plain and ordinary ſenſe of the words of this oath, without any evaſion, equivocation, or mental reſervation whatever, and without any diſpenſation already granted by the Pope, or any authority of the See of Rome, or any perſon whatever; and without thinking that I am or can be acquitted before God or man, or abſolved of this declaration, or any part thereof, although the Pope, or any other perſon or perſons, or authority whatſoever, ſhall diſpenſe with, or annul the ſame, or declare that it was null and void from the beginning.

"So help me God."

And be it enacted by the authority aforeſaid, that the officer of the Court of King's Bench, juſtices of the peace, and magiſtrates of the city and towns corporate, ſhall yearly, within twenty-one days after the firſt of December, return to the Clerk of the Privy Council of this kingdom, or his deputy, a true and perfect liſt, under his or their hand, of every ſuch Papiſt as ſhall in the courſe of the preceding year have taken and ſubſcribed ſuch oath, in which liſt the quality, condition, title, and place of abode of ſuch Papiſt ſhall be ſpecified.

About

About the ſame time, fearing that their grievances were not known to his Majeſty, the Catholics prepared a Petition; which was preſented to Lord Buckinghamſhire by Lord Fingal, Mr. Preſton and Mr. Dermot, in order that it might be tranſmitted by him to the King.*

To the King's moſt Excellent Majeſty, the humble Addreſs and Petition of the Roman Catholics of Ireland.

Moſt Gracious Sovereign,

We your Majeſty's moſt dutiful ſubjects, the Roman Catholics of your kingdom of Ireland, with hearts full of loyalty, but overwhelmed with affliction, and depreſſed by our calamitous and ruined circumſtances, beg leave to lay at your Majeſty's feet ſome ſmall part of thoſe numerous and inſupportable grievances under which we have long groaned, not only without any act of diſobedience, but even without murmur or complaint; in hopes that our inviolable ſubmiſſion, and unaltered patience under thoſe ſevere preſſures, would fully confute the accuſation of ſeditious principles, with which we have been unfortunately and unjuſtly charged.

We are deeply ſenſible of your Majeſty's clemency, in moderating the rigorous execution of ſome of the laws againſt us: but we humbly beg leave to repreſent, that ſeveral, and thoſe the moſt ſevere and diſtreſſing of thoſe laws, *execute themſelves with the moſt fatal certainty*, and that your Majeſty's clemency cannot, in the ſmalleſt degree, interpoſe for their

* This address was written by Mr. Burke.

their mitigation, otherwiſe your Roman Catholic ſubjects would moſt chearfully acquieſce in that reſource, and reſt with an abſolute and unbounded aſſurance, on your Majeſty's princely generoſity, and your pious regard to the rights of private conſcience.

We are, may it pleaſe your Majeſty, a numerous and very induſtrious part of your Majeſty's ſubjects, and yet by no induſtry, by no honeſt endeavours on our part, is it in our power to acquire or to hold, almoſt any ſecure or permanent property whatſoever; we are not only diſqualified to purchaſe, but are diſabled from occupying any land even in farm, except on a tenure extremely ſcanted both in profit and in time; and if we ſhould venture to expend any thing on the melioration of land thus held, by building, by incloſure, by draining, or by any other ſpecies of improvement, ſo very neceſſary in this country; ſo far would our ſervices be bettering our fortunes, that theſe are preciſely the very circumſtances, which, as the law now ſtands, muſt neceſſarily diſqualify us from continuing thoſe farms, for any time in our poſſeſſion.

Whilſt the endeavours of our induſtry are thus diſcouraged, (no leſs, we humbly apprehend, to the detriment of the national proſperity and the diminution of your Majeſty's revenue, than to our particular ruin) there are a ſet of men, who, inſtead of exerciſing any honeſt occupation in the commonwealth, make it their employment to pry into our miſerable property, to drag us into the courts, and to compel us to confeſs on our oaths, and under the penalties of perjury, whether we have, in any inſtance, acquired a property in the ſmalleſt degree exceeding what the rigour of the law has admitted; and in ſuch caſe the informers, without any other merit than that of their diſcovery, are inveſted (to the daily ruin of ſeveral innocent, induſtrious families) not only with the ſurplus

in

in which the law is exceeded, but in the whole body of the eſtate, and intereſt ſo diſcovered, and it is our grief that this evil is likely to continue and increaſe, as informers have, in this country, almoſt worn off the infamy, which in all ages, and in all other countries, has attended their character, and have grown into ſome repute by the frequency and ſucceſs of their practices.

And this, moſt gracious Sovereign, though extremely grievous, is far from being the only or moſt oppreſſive particular, in which our diſtreſs is connected with the breach of the rules of honour and morality. By the laws now in force in this kingdom, a ſon, however undutiful or profligate, ſhall, merely by the merit of conforming to the eſtabliſhed religion, deprive the Roman Catholic father of that free and full poſſeſſion of his eſtate, that power to mortgage or otherwiſe diſpoſe of it, as the exigencies of his affairs may require; but ſhall himſelf have full liberty immediately to mortgage or otherwiſe alienate the reverſion of that eſtate, from his family for ever; a regulation by which a father, contrary to the order of nature, is put under the power of his ſon, and through which an early diſſoluteneſs is not only ſuffered, but encouraged, by giving a pernicious privilege, the frequent uſe of which has broken the hearts of many deſerving parents, and entailed poverty and deſpair on ſome of the moſt ancient and opulent families in this kingdom.

Even when the parent has the good fortune to eſcape this calamity in his life-time, yet he has at his death, the melancholy and almoſt certain proſpect of leaving neither peace nor fortune to his children; for by that law, which beſtows the whole fortune on the firſt conformiſt, or, on non-conformity, diſperſes it among the children, incurable jealouſies and animoſities have ariſen; a total extinction of principle and of

natural

natural benevolence has enſued; whilſt we are obliged to conſider our own offspring and the brothers of our own blood, as our moſt dangerous enemies; the bleſſing of providence on our families, in a numerous iſſue, is converted into the moſt certain means of their ruin and depravation: we are, moſt gracious Sovereign, neither permitted to enjoy the few broken remains of our patrimonial inheritance, nor by our induſtry to acquire any ſecure eſtabliſhment to our families.

In this deplorable ſituation, let it not be conſidered, we earneſtly beſeech your Majeſty, as an inſtance of preſumption or diſcontent, that we thus adventure to lay open to your Majeſty's mercy, a very ſmall part of our uncommon ſufferings; what we have concealed under a reſpectful ſilence, would form a far longer, and full as melancholy a recital; we ſpeak with reluctance, though we feel with anguiſh; we reſpect from the bottom of our hearts that legiſlation under which we ſuffer; but we humbly conceive it is impoſſible to procure redreſs without complaint, or to make a complaint, that by ſome conſtruction may not appear to convey blame: and nothing, we aſſure your Majeſty, ſhould have extorted from us even theſe complaints, but the ſtrong neceſſity we find ourſelves under of employing every lawful, humble endeavour, leſt the whole purpoſe of our lives and labours ſhould prove only the means of confirming to ourſelves, and entailing on our poſterity, inevitable beggary, and the moſt abject ſervitude; a ſervitude the more intolerable, as it is ſuffered amidſt that liberty, that peace, and that ſecurity, which, under your Majeſty's benign influence, is ſpread all around us, and which we alone, of all your Majeſty's ſubjects, are rendered incapable of partaking.

In all humility we implore, that our principles may not be eſtimated by the inflamed charge of controverſial writers, nor

our

our practices measured by the events of those troubled periods, when parties have run high (though these have been often misrepresented, and always cruelly exaggerated to our prejudice); but that we may be judged by our own actions, and in our own times; and we humbly offer it to your most equitable and princely consideration, that we do not rest the proof of our sincerity on words, but on things; on our dutiful, peaceable, submissive behaviour for more than fourscore years: and though it will be considered as too severe to form any opinion of great bodies, by the practice of individuals, *yet if in all that time, amongst all our people, in the daily increase of severe laws against us, one treasonable insurrection, or one treasonable conspiracy can be proved; if amongst our clergy, one seditious sermon can be shewn to have been preached;* we will readily admit that there is good reason for continuing the present laws in all their force against us; but if, on the contrary, (we speak in full confidence), it can be shewn, that our clergy have ever exerted their utmost endeavours to enforce submission to your Majesty's government, and obedience to your laws; if it can be shewn that these endeavours have always been most strenuous in times of public danger, or when any accident tended to create a ferment amongst the people; if our laity have frequently offered (what we are always ready to fulfil) to hazard their lives and fortunes for your Majesty's service; if we have willingly bound up the fruits of our discouraged industry with the fortune of your Majesty's government in the public loans; then, we humbly hope, we may be admitted to a small portion of mercy, and that that behaviour, which your Majesty's benignity and condescension will esteem a merit in our circumstances, may entitle us, not to reward, but to such toleration as may enable us to become useful citizens to our country, and subjects as profitable, as we are loyal to your Majesty.

Permit

Permit us, most gracious Sovereign, on this occasion, to reiterate the assurances of our unshaken loyalty, which all our sufferings have not been able to abate; of our sincere zeal for your Majesty's service, of our attachment to the constitution of our country, and of our warmest gratitude for your Majesty's continual indulgence, and for the late instance of favour we have experienced from Parliament, in enabling us, consistent with our religious tenets, to give a legal proof of our sentiments upon these points. And we humbly hope, that the alacrity and eagerness with which we have seized this first, though long wished opportunity of testifying, in the most solemn and public manner, our inviolable fidelity to your Majesty, our real principles, and our good-will and affection towards our fellow-subjects, will extinguish all jealousies, and remove those imputations, which alone have hitherto held us forth in the light of enemies to your Majesty, and to the state. And if any thing farther can be suggested or devised, whereby we can, by our actions, more fully evince our sincerity, we shall consider such an opportunity of demonstrating our real loyalty, as an high favour, and shall be deficient in no act whatever, which does not amount to a renunciation of that religious profession which we value more than our lives, and which it cannot be suspected we hold from obstinacy or a contempt of the laws, since it has not been taken up by ourselves, but has, from time immemorial, been handed down to us from our ancestors.

We derive no small consolation, most gracious Sovereign, from considering, that the most severe and rigorous of the laws against us had been enacted before the accession of your Majesty's most illustrious House to the Throne of these kingdoms: we therefore indulge the more sanguine hopes, that the mitigation of them, and the establishment of peace, industry, and universal happiness, amongst all your loyal subjects, may be one of the bleſſings of your Majeſty's reign. *And though we might plead in favour of ſuch relaxation, the expreſs words of a ſolemn treaty, entered into with us, by your Majeſty's royal predeceſſor, King William, (which has been forfeited by no diſobedience on our part)*, yet we neither wiſh, nor deſire, to receive any thing, but as a mere act of your Majeſty's clemency, and of the indulgence and equity of your Parliament.

That this act of truly loyal beneficence and juſtice may be added to the other inſtances of your Majeſty's auguſt virtues, and that the deliverance of a faithful and diſtreſſed people may be one of thoſe diſtinguiſhing acts of your reign, which ſhall tranſmit its memory to the love, gratitude, and veneration, of our lateſt poſterity, is the humble prayer of, &c. &c.

In the year 1778,* an act paſſed "for the "relief of his Majeſty's ſubjects of this king-"dom, profeſſing the Popiſh religion." The preamble of which contains a confirmation of every thing that has been already advanced, concerning the loyalty of the Catholics, and a declaration on the part of the King and Parliament, concerning the policy of admitting the Catholics into a full participation of the bleſſings of the Conſtitution, which is a complete recognition of their right to enjoy them. It ſtates, "And "Whereas, from their uniform peaceable beha-"viour

* 17th and 18th of Geo. III. c. 49.

"viour for a long ſeries of years, it appears
"reaſonable and expedient to relax the ſame,
"(the laws of Anne); and it muſt tend not
"only to the cultivation and improvement of this
"kingdom, but to the proſperity and ſtrength of
"all his Majeſty's dominions, *that his ſubjects of*
"*all denominations, ſhould enjoy the bleſſings of a*
"*free conſtitution, and ſhould be bound to each other*
"*by mutual intereſt and mutual affection, &c.*"

By this act Papiſts, provided they take the oath of declaration of 13th and 14th of Geo. III. c. 35, are admitted to the following privileges.— They may take land on leaſes not exceeding 999 years, or determinable upon any number of lives not exceeding five.

The lands of Papiſts are to be deſcendable, deviſeable, and transferable, as fully as if the ſame were in the ſeizure of any other of his Majeſty's ſubjects.

Papiſts are rendered capable to hold and enjoy all eſtates which may deſcend, be deviſed or transferred to them.

No

No maintenance is to be hereafter granted to a conforming child of a Papiſt, out of the perſonal property of ſuch Papiſt, except out of ſuch leaſes as which may be taken under this act.

And the conformity of the eldeſt ſon is not to alter hereafter the Popiſh parents eſtate.

In the year 1782, another act paſſed "for "the further relief of his Majeſty's ſubjects "of this kingdom, profeſſing the Popiſh re- "ligion."*

The preamble of this act ſtates: "Whereas, "all ſuch of his Majeſty's ſubjects in this king- "dom, of whatever perſuaſion, as have here- "tofore taken and ſubſcribed, or ſhall hereafter "take and ſubſcribe, the oath of allegiance and "declaration preſcribed by an act paſſed in the "13th and 14th year of his preſent Majeſty's "reign, entitled an act to enable his Majeſty's "ſubjects, of whatever perſuaſion, to teſtify their "allegiance to him, ought to be conſidered as "good

* 21st and 22d Geo. III. c. 24.

" good and loyal ſubjects to his Majeſty, his " crown and government: and whereas a con- " tinuance of ſeveral of the laws formerly " enacted, and ſtill in force in this kingdom, " againſt perſons profeſſing the popiſh religion, " is therefore unneceſſary, in reſpect to thoſe " who have taken, or ſhall take the ſaid oath, " and is injurious to the real wealth and proſ- " perity of Ireland, therefore, &c.

By this act Catholics, provided they take this oath, may purchaſe or take lands, or any intereſt therein, except advowſons or boroughs returning members of Parliament, and diſpoſe of the ſame by will or otherwiſe; and Popiſh eccleſiaſtics, on the ſame condition, and regiſtering their name and abode, with the regiſter of the dioceſe, are diſcharged from all penalties.

This act repeals ſo much of 8th Anne, as ſub- jects Papiſts to fine and impriſonment, on his refuſal to teſtify on oath before two juſtices of the peace, when and where he heard the Popiſh maſs celebrated, and the names of the perſons celebrating it; and ſo much of 7th Wm. III. c. 5.

as ſubjects any Papiſt, who ſhall have in his poſſeſſion any horſe of the value of 5l. or more, to the penalties therein mentioned; and ſo much of 8th Anne, as enables the Lord Lieutenant to ſeize any horſe belonging to a Papiſt, upon a proſpect of invaſion or rebellion. It alſo repeals ſo much of 9th Geo. II. c. 6. as enables grand juries to reimburſe ſuch perſons who have been robbed by privateers in time of war, for their loſſes, and to levy the ſame on the goods of Papiſts only; and ſo much of 6th Geo. I. c. 10. as ſubjects Papiſts, who ſhall not provide a Proteſtant watchman to watch in their turn, to certain penalties; and ſo much of 2d Anne, c. 6, as ſubjects Papiſts, who took any houſe, or came to dwell in Limerick, after the year 1703, or within the town of Galway, to certain penalties.

In the ſame year was likewiſe paſſed an act to allow perſons, profeſſing the Popiſh religion, to teach ſchool in this kingdom, and for regulating the education of Papiſts, and alſo to repeal parts of certain laws relative to the guardianſhip of their children.*

The

* 21st and 22d Geo. III. c. 62.

The preamble ſtates: "Whereas ſeveral of the "laws made in this kingdom, relative to the edu- "cation of Papiſts, or perſons profeſſing the "Popiſh religion, are conſidered as too ſevere, "and have not anſwered the deſired effect."

This act repeals ſo much of 7th Wm. III. c. 4. and 8th of Anne, c. 3. as ſubjects Catholics, who ſhall publicly teach ſchool, or privately inſtruct youth, to the like penalties as any Popiſh regular convict, provided they take the oaths of 13th and 14th of George III. c. 35; and it enables Catholics, except eccleſiaſtics, to be guardians.

Of the numerous individuals, who at this time diſtinguiſhed themſelves for their exertions in favour of the Catholics, there was no one to whom they were under greater obligations than to the late Mr. Burke. He wrote for them the Petition which was preſented to the King in 1774. In the Engliſh Houſe of Commons in 1778 he was the firſt to declare the neceſſity of conceſſions being made to them; he ſaid that "Ireland was "now the chief dependence of the Britiſh crown,

" and that it particularly behoved that country to " admit the Irish nation to the privileges of Bri- " tish citizens;"* and, in the year 1782, he wrote his celebrated letter to Lord Kenmare, in which he so ably exposes the folly, injustice, and tyranny of the penal laws.

It certainly is a fact of no small importance in favour of the wisdom of unlimited concession to the Catholics, that this great statesman, the advocate for existing establishments, and who was the first and most formidable opponent to the progress of the jacobinical principles of France, should have advised it, and incessantly forwarded it by his powerful talents and extensive influence.

But the Catholics were indebted, not only to the labours of their friends, but also to the great revolution which was going on at this period in America, for the success of the first concessions that were made to them. This appears very evident, from the failure of an attempt which was made

* 8th Eng. Deb. p. 185, 1st April, 1778.

made by Mr. James Fitzgerald, a few months before the introduction of the act of 17. 18. Geo. III. to obtain for them a power to take leases for lands for 61 years. For, soon afterwards, when the intelligence arrived of the defeat of the British forces in America, the same Parliament, on the recommendation of the government, passed an act for enabling them to take land on leases for 999 years.

It was not, however, till the British government were obliged to transport the whole of the British army from Ireland to America, and thus leave it exposed to the attacks of France, that the Catholics became of sufficient importance in the eyes either of their own Protestant countrymen, or of the British government, to be attended to and caressed by them. The only alternative then left for the Protestants to adopt, was either to promote a union of sects in the common defence of the kingdom, or to make up their minds to fall an easy prey to the arms of France. Upon this principle of preservation, by an oblivion of all past animosities, the volunteers were embodied, and composed indiscriminately of Catholics and Protestants.

Proteſtants. But, in proportion as the danger of invaſion diminiſhed, they naturally turned their attention to the grievances that both ſects experienced at the hands of the Britiſh government, and ſoon became an armed aſſociation for the attainment of political rights.

In this appeal to arms, in open reſiſtance to the power of Great Britain, for the purpoſe of compelling her to grant to Ireland the independence of her legiſlature, and a reform of her Parliament, the Proteſtants took the lead. But the contention between them and the Britiſh government was not one of arms, becauſe Great Britain had no troops with which to diſpute with the volunteers, but one of political manœuvring. It was plain, that to which ever party the Catholics attached themſelves, victory would belong. The government, therefore, in order to ſecure them, paſſed the acts of 1778 and 1782; while the Proteſtants, on the other hand, endeavoured to conciliate them by public reſolutions and declarations in favour of their complete emancipation. The Dungannon convention, which met in February 1782, and was compoſed of the repreſentatives of

143 Proteſtant corps of volunteers, reſolved, with two diſſenting voices only, "that they held the "right of private judgment, in matters of religion, "to be equally ſacred in others as themſelves; "therefore, that, as Chriſtians and Proteſtants, "they rejoiced in the relaxation of the penal laws "againſt their Roman Catholic fellow-ſubjects, "and that they conceived the meaſure to be "fraught with the happieſt conſequences to the "union and proſperity of Ireland."

Theſe liberal declarations on the part of this meeting, and the general tenor of the conduct of the Proteſtants throughout Ireland towards the Catholics, ſecured their cordial concurrence, and the Britiſh Government were, at length, reluctantly obliged to concede the favourite object of an independent Iriſh legiſlature.

The Proteſtants now proceeded to attempt to carry their other great object, a parliamentary reform; and, after the ſenſe of the kingdom had been expreſſed, at various public meetings, to be decidedly in favour of it, they determined to hold a convention in Dublin, for the purpoſe of impreſſing

preſſing upon government and parliament the neceſſity of acceding to their demands.* In the mean time, a diviſion of opinion had manifeſted itſelf among ſome of the northern corps of volunteers on the Catholic queſtion, and Lord Charlemont and other perſons had declared themſelves hoſtile to further conceſſions. This circumſtance afforded the government an eaſy opportunity of defeating the object of the convention; they contrived to have a motion made for connecting the emancipation of the Catholics with the queſtion of parliamentary reform; and upon its being rejected by the convention, knowing that its power was not to be dreaded, if unſupported by the Catholic population, they deſpiſed its threats, and, by a manly oppoſition to their demands, they ſecured their diſperſion without tumult, and certainly without the regret of the advocates of ſuch a reform in Parliament as the general circumſtances of the country abſolutely required.

From this period, to the year 1790, the Catholic queſtion was not once agitated, either by the Catholics or by Parliament. In this year the attorney-

* This convention met in Dublin in 1784.

torney-general brought in a bill to explain and amend the act of 22d Geo. III. c. 62.

The intention of this act was to give to Catholics the power of appointing guardians to their children, but it was so carelessly drawn, that, upon consulting it, in the case of the will of the late Lord Gormanstown, by which he had appointed guardians to his son, it was discovered that they were not competent to act. The present bill was therefore introduced to remedy this defect.

A circumstance, which took place this summer shews, that this act of common justice was not, in any degree, the result of an inclination, on the part of government, to treat the Catholics with more than customary liberality: Lord Westmoreland, then Lord Lieutenant, had visited the South of Ireland; and, on his arrival at Cork, it was intimated to the Catholics there, that an expression of their loyalty would be acceptable. Accordingly an address of that nature was prepared, which, however, concluded with a *hope*, that their loyalty would entitle them to some relaxation of the penal

code.

code. Before its being formally presented, it was submitted to his Excellency, and was returned to them, to strike out the clause which expressed hope. With a feeling rather natural to men not perfectly broken down by oppression, they refused to strike it out, and declined presenting the address.

A century of pains and penalties had now elapsed, in which period the most severe and minute investigation had not been able to ascribe to the Catholics one instance of disloyalty, when they at length determined to make a vigorous exertion to obtain a restoration of their constitutional rights. In the course of the year 1790, violent resolutions had been entered into by the magistrates of the county of Armagh against them. Those of Dublin, and of the other principal cities and towns of Ireland, were in consequence roused to adopt resolutions on their part, expressive of the necessity of petitioning Parliament. These had been transmitted to the general committee of Catholics, who thereupon held a meeting to consider them on the 11th of February 1791. The general committee referred these resolutions to a sub-

committee,

committee, who made upon them the following report:

"Your committee having, in obedience to "your directions, carefully perufed the refolutions "of the Catholics of Ireland, report, that faid re- "folutions contain the moft unequivocal fenti- "ments of loyalty to our moft gracious Sove- "reign, George the Third, of love for our coun- "try, and obedience to its laws, and the moft "humble hope of being reftored to fome partici- "pation of its excellent conftitution.

"That your Catholic brethren refer, with con- "fidence, to the numberlefs proofs they have "given of fidelity in times the moft perilous, "when rebellion raged in the bofom of Britain, "and when foreign invafion threatened our coaft, "and to that alacrity with which all defcriptions "of our people took the oath of allegiance; "and they rely that their fcrupulous obfervance "of fuch facred obligation will no where be "doubted, when it is confidered, that if they "took thofe oaths required by law, they would

" thereby become entitled to all the rights of " citizens.

" That, with all humility, they confide in the " justice, liberality, and wisdom of Parliament, " and the benignity of our most gracious Sove- " reign, to relieve them from their degraded situa- " tion, and no longer to suffer them to continue " like strangers in their native land; but thus " have the glory of shewing all Europe, that in " the plenitude of power, strength, and riches of " the British empire, when nothing they grant " can be imputed to any motives but those of jus- " tice and toleration; that, at such a period, they " deign to hear and relieve their oppressed and " faithful subjects, and to unite them for ever to " their country, by every tie of gratitude and in- " terest; and that they will shew to all Europe, " that humble and peaceful conduct, and dutiful " application, are the only true and effectual me- " thods for good subjects to obtain relief from a " wise and good government.

" That our Catholic brethren therefore desire, " that application may be made for such relief as " the

" the wisdom and justice of Parliament may grant;
" and they hope to be restored, at least, to some
" of the rights and privileges which have been
" wisely granted to others who dissent from the
" established church; that they may be thus
" enabled to promote, in conjunction with the rest
" of their fellow-subjects, the present and future
" happiness and strength of their country.

" That our said Catholic brethren direct, that
" such application be immediately made, and con-
" tinued, in the most submissive and constitutional
" manner, for a mitigation of the restrictions and
" disqualifications under which they labour."

The general committee having agreed with and adopted this report, a petition was prepared in order to be laid before Parliament in the ensuing session.

With this petition a deputation of the general committee waited upon the chief Secretary, Lord Hobart, to solicit the countenance and protection of government, but in vain. This was not only refused them, but the Catholics of Ireland,

 constituting,

constituting, at the lowest calculation, three fourths of the inhabitants of the kingdom, had not even sufficient influence to induce any one member of Parliament to present it.

A second deputation having failed to obtain even an answer from government to a renewed application for its support, it was determined to send Mr. Keogh to London, to lay before his Majesty's Ministers the state of his Catholic subjects.

Mr. Keogh, on his arrival in London, instituted a negociation with Mr. Pitt and the Cabinet; at the close of which, the Catholics were given to understand that they might hope for four objects—grand juries, county magistrates, high sheriffs, and the bar. Admission to the right of suffrage was also mentioned, and taken under consideration.

The spirit of religious liberty having, at this time, made great progress among the Protestant dissenters in Ulster, the 1st Belfast volunteer company, in July 1791, passed a resolution in favour of of admitting the Catholics a full enjoyment of the conſtitution; and, in October, the great Northern Aſſociation of United Iriſhmen* pledged themſelves "to endeavour, by all due means, to pro-"cure a complete and radical reform of the "people in Parliament, including Iriſhmen of "every religious perſuaſion."

In the mean time, whilſt Mr. Keogh was in London, the Iriſh Adminiſtration had been endeavouring to counteract the views of the Catholic body, by a negociation with the principal nobility and gentry belonging to it; and, in ſome degree, their exertions were ſucceſsful. For, at a meeting of the general committee, held in December 1791, for the purpoſe of conſidering of the policy of petitioning Parliament in the enſuing ſeſſion, ſome of the meeting wiſhed to adopt a reſolution of ſeeking no removal of the exiſting diſabilities, but in ſuch a manner and to ſuch an extent as the wiſdom of the legiſlature deemed expedient. This was reſiſted by others, and, on a diviſion

* It was not till 1794, that a new ſociety, under this name, embarked in an attempt to ſeparate Great Britain and Ireland.

a division upon the queſtion of petitioning, the nobility were left in a minority of 90 to 17.

Purſuant to this deciſion, the following petition was drawn up, and introduced into the Houſe of Commons, by Mr. O'Hara, on the 23d January, 1792.

We your petitioners, being appointed by ſundry of his Majeſty's ſubjects profeſſing the Roman Catholic religion, to be agents for conducting applications to the legiſlature for their relief, in our own and their names, beg leave to approach this High Court of Parliament with an unfeigned reſpect for its wiſdom and authority; and, at the ſame time, with a deep and heartfelt ſenſation of our ſingular and deplorable ſituation. And, firſt of all, we implore (and for this we throw ourſelves on the indulgence of Parliament) that no irregularity or defect in form or language, ſhould obſtruct the ſucceſs of theſe our moſt ardent ſupplications. The circumſtances in which we ſtand deſerve conſideration. For near a hundred years, we and our fathers, and our grandfathers, have groaned under a code of laws, (in ſome parts already purged from the ſtatutes), the like of which, no age, no nation, no climate ever ſaw. Yet, ſore as it were from the ſcourge of active perſecution, ſcarce yet confirmed in our minds, and but lately ſecure in our perſons and in our houſes, from the daily alarms of ſearch-warrants and informers, we come before Parliament for the firſt time; and we come to aſk an alleviation of burdens, under which we can only find conſolation in the melancholy compariſon of former times. In this ſtate of recent apprehenſion

prehenſion and troubled anxious hope, with minds unadapted to the preciſe obſervances of decorum, we reſt upon the ſimple merits of our caſe It is a part of our calamities, that we do not know how to tell them with propriety; and if our complaints ſhould deviate into remonſtrance, and we ſhould ſeem to upbraid, when we mean to ſupplicate, we truſt a due allowance will be made for expreſſions extorted by our anguiſh, or proceeding from an inevitable ignorance of form. Excluded from the conſtitution in all its parts, and in many reſpects aliens to the law, how ſhould we have learned the forms of Parliament?

The hardſhips we ſuffer proceed from the law. It is, therefore, only to the fountain of the law that we can look for relief. You are the great Council of our Sovereign Lord the King; but you are alſo ſubjects like ourſelves. The ear of Majeſty, by the law of the land, and by the benignity of that Sovereign, whom it is your glory to imitate, is ever open to the petitions of his people. As far as we are able to diſcern the great outlines of a conſtitution, which we know only in ſpeculation, we conceive that it is the boaſt of the conſtitution of theſe kingdoms, to have aſſociated a portion of the people into the Sovereign power; in order that, not dazzled by the awe of ſupreme Majeſty, the ſubject may find a happy mediatorial inſtitution, an aſylum wherein to depoſit the burden of his griefs, to expoſe the nakedneſs of his oppreſſions, and indulge complaint even to exaggeration. There were, indeed, thoſe who would have made us believe, that Parliament was only to be approached with circumſpect and timid ſteps; at moſt, in general terms; and that, wrapped in proud and inexorable ſtate, you would conſider a ſpecification of the wants of the people as an inſult, and a reaſon for not ſupplying them. But we knew it could not be. We knew that no ſenate, no king, no tyrant, had ever profeſſed

to

to turn his ear from detailed ſupplication. The Majeſty of God himſelf is willing to receive, and demands the incenſe of particular prayer. And ſhall we, who ſpeak from man to man, from ſubject to ſubject, not dare to ſpecify the meaſure and extent of our crying neceſſities. Deſpiſing that baſe and hypocritical affectation, we are ſure it is far more congenial to the nature and to the temper of Parliament, with a firm and generous confidence, to ſay, as we ſay—here is the evil—there is the remedy: To you we look for relief.

Behold us then before you, three millions of the people of Ireland, ſubjects of the ſame king, inhabitants of the ſame land, bound together by the ſame ſocial contract, contributing to the ſame revenues, defended by the ſame armies, declared, by the authentic words of an act of Parliament, to be good and loyal ſubjects to his Majeſty, his Crown, and Government, and yet doomed to one general unqualified incapacity, an univerſal excluſion, an univerſal civil proſcription. We are excluded from the ſtate, we are excluded from the revenues. We are excluded from every diſtinction, every privilege, every office, every emolument, every civil truſt, every corporate right. We are excluded from the navy, from the army, from the magiſtrature, from the profeſſions. We are excluded from the palladium of life, liberty, and property, the juries and inqueſts of our country.—From what are we not excluded? We are excluded from the conſtitution. We ſtand a ſtrange anomaly in the law; not acknowledged, not diſavowed; not ſlaves, not freemen: an exception to the principles of juriſprudence; a prodigy in the ſyſtem of civil inſtitution. We incur no ſmall part of the penalties of a general outlawry, and a general excommunication. Diſability meets us at every hour, and in every walk of life. It cramps our induſtry, it ſhackles our property, it depreſſes our genius, it debilitates our minds.—Why are we diſfranchiſed, and why are we degraded? Or rather, why do these evils afflict our country, of which we are no inconsiderable part?

We most humbly and earnestly supplicate and implore Parliament to call this law of universal exclusion to a severe account, and now at last to demand of it, upon what principle it stands, of equity, of morality, of justice, or of policy. And, while we request this scrutiny into the law, we demand also the severest scrutiny into our principles, our actions, our words, and our thoughts. Wherein have we failed as loyal and affectionate subjects to the best of Sovereigns, or as sober, peaceable, and useful members of society. Where is that people who can offer the testimony of a hundred years patient submission to a code of laws, of which no man living is now an advocate—without sedition, without murmur, without complaint. Our loyalty has undergone a century of severe persecution for the sake of our religion, and we have come out of the ordeal with our religion, and with our loyalty.

Why then are we still left under the ban of our country? We differ, it is true, from the national church, in some points of doctrinal faith. Whether it is our blessing or our misfortune, He only knows to whom all things are known. For this our religion we offer no apology. After ages of learned and critical discussion, we cannot expect to throw farther light upon it. We have only to say, that it is founded on revelation, as well as the religion established by law. Both you and we are regenerated in the same baptism, and profess our belief in the same Christ; you according to the church of England, we according to the church of Rome. We do not exercise an abject or obscure superstition. If we err, our errors have been, and still are, sanctioned by the example of many flourishing, learned, and civilized nations. We do not enter, we disdain to enter into the cavils of antiquated sophistry, and to insult the understanding of Parliament by supposing

ing it neceſſary to prove that a religion is not incompatible with civil government, which has ſubſiſted for ſo many hundred years under every poſſible form of government, in ſome tolerated, in ſome eſtabliſhed, even to this day.

With regard to our civil principles, we are unalterably, deeply, and zealouſly attached to his Majeſty's perſon and government. Good and loyal ſubjects we are, and we are declared by law to be. With regard to the Conſtitution of the state, we are as much attached to it as it is poſſible for men to be attached to a conſtitution by which they are not avowed. With regard to the conſtitution of the church, we are, indeed, inviolably attached to our own: Firſt, becauſe we believe it to be true; and next, becauſe, beyond belief, we know that its principles are calculated to make us, and have made us, good men and good citizens. But as we find it anſwers to us, individually, all the uſeful ends of religion, *we ſolemnly and conſcientiouſly declare, that we are ſatisfied with the preſent condition of our eccleſiaſtical policy. With ſatisfaction, we acquieſce in the eſtabliſhment of the national church; we neither repine at its poſſeſſions, nor envy its dignities; we are ready, upon this point, to give every aſſurance that is binding upon man.*

With regard to every other ſubject, and to every other calumny, we have no diſavowals, we have no declarations to make: Conſcious of the innocence of our lives, and the purity of our intentions, we are juſtified in aſking, what reaſon of ſtate exiſts, and we deny that any does exiſt, for leaving us ſtill in the bondage of the law, and under the protracted reſtriction of penal ſtatutes. Penalties ſuppoſe, if not crimes, at leaſt a cauſe of reaſonable ſuſpicion. Criminal imputations like thoſe (for to be adequate to the effect, they muſt be great indeed) are, to a generous mind, more grievous than the penalties themſelves. They incontrovertibly imply, that we

are

are confidered by the legiflature as ftanding in a doubtful light of fidelity or loyalty to the King, or to the conftitution of our country, and perhaps to both. While on thefe unjuft fuppofitions we are deprived of the common rights and privileges of Britifh and of Irifh fubjects, it is impoffible for us to fay we are contented while we endure a relentlefs civil profcription for which no caufe is alleged, and for which no reafon can be affigned.

Becaufe we now come with a clear, open, and manly voice, to infift upon the grievances under which we ftill labour, it is not to be inferred that we have forgot the benignant juftice of Parliament, which has relieved us from the more oppreffive, but not the moft extenfive part of the penal fyftem. In thofe days of affliction, when we lay proftrate under the iron rod, and, as it were, entranced in a gulph of perfecution, it was neceffary for Parliament to go the whole way, and to ftretch out a faving hand to relieve us. We had not the courage to look up with hope, to know our condition, or even to conceive a remedy. It is becaufe the former relaxations were not thrown away upon us; it is becaufe we begin to feel the influence of fomewhat more equal laws, and to revive from our former inanition, that we now prefume to ftand erect before you: Conceiving that Parliament has a right to expect, as a teft of our gratitude, that we fhould no longer lie a dead weight upon our country, but come forward in our turn to affift with our voice, our exertions, and our councils, in a work, to which the wifdom and power of Parliament is incompetent without our co-operation—the application of a policy, wholly new, to the preffing wants, and to the intimate neceffities of a people long forgotten, out of the fight and out of the knowledge of a fuperintending legiflature.—Accordingly we are come, and we claim no fmall merit that we have found our way to the door of Parliament. It has not been made eafy for us.—Every art and induftry has been exerted to

 obftruct

obſtruct us: Attempts have been made to divide us into factions, and to throw us into confuſion. We have ſtood firm and united. We have received hints and cautions; obſcure intimations and public warnings to guard our ſupplications againſt intimidation. We have reſiſted that ſpecies of diſguiſed and artful threat. We have been traduced, calumniated, and libelled. We have witneſſed ſiniſter endeavours again to blow the flame of religious animoſity, and awake the ſlumbering ſpirit of popular terrors and popular fury.—But we have remained unmoved. We are, indeed, accuſtomed to this tumid agitation and ferment in the public mind. In former times it was the conſtant precurſor of more intenſe perſecution, but it has alſo attended every later and happier return of legiſlative mercy. But whether it betokens us evil or good, to Parliament we come, to ſeek, at that ſhrine, a ſafeguard from impending danger, or a communication of new benefits.

What then do we aſk of Parliament? To be thoroughly united and made one with the reſt of our fellow-ſubjects. That, alas! would be our firſt, our deareſt wiſh. But if that is denied us, if ſacrifices are to be made, if by an example of rare moderation, we do not aſpire to the condition of a fair equality, we are not at a loſs to find, in the range of ſocial benefits (which is nearly that of our preſent excluſions) an object which is, and ought to be, the ſcope and reſting-place of our wiſhes and our hopes. That which, if we do not aſk, we are not worthy to obtain. We knock that it may be opened unto us. We have learned by tradition from our anceſtors, we have heard by fame in foreign lands, where we have been driven to ſeek education in youth, and bread in manhood; and, by the contemplation of our own minds, we are filled with a deep and unalterable opinion that the Iriſh, formed upon the model of the Britiſh conſtitution, is a bleſſing of ineſtimable value; that it contributes, and is even eſſentially neceſſary for national and individual happineſs. Of this conſtitution, we feel ourſelves worthy; and though not practically, we know the benefits of its franchiſes. Nor can we, without a crimimal diſſimulation, conceal from Parliament the painful inquietude which is felt by our whole perſuaſion, and the dangers to which we do not ceaſe to be expoſed, by this our total and unmerited excluſion from the common rights, privileges, and franchiſes, conceded by our Kings for the protection of the ſubject. This excluſion is indeed the root of every evil. It is that which makes property inſecure, and induſtry precarious. It pollutes the ſtream of juſtice. It is the cauſe of daily humiliation. It is the inſurmountable barrier, the impaſſible line of ſeparation which divides the nation, and which, keeping animoſity alive, prevents the entire and cordial intermixture of the people. And therefore inevitably it is, that ſome ſhare, ſome portion, ſome participation in the liberties and franchiſes of our country, becomes the primary and eſſential object of our ardent and common ſolicitation. It is a bleſſing for which there is no price, and can be no compenſation. With it, every evil is tolerable; without it, no advantage is deſirable. In this, as in all things, we ſubmit ourſelves to the paramount authority of Parliament; and we ſhall acquieſce in what is given, as we do in what is taken away. But this is the boon we aſk. We hunger and we thirſt for the conſtitution of our country. If it ſhall be deemed otherwiſe, and ſhall be determined that we are qualified perhaps for the baſe and lucrative tenures of profeſſional occupation, but unworthy to perform the free and noble ſervices of the conſtitution, we ſubmit, indeed, but we ſolemnly proteſt againſt that diſtinction for ourſelves and for our children. It is no act of ours. Whatever judgment may await our merits or our failings, we cannot conclude ourſelves, by recognizing, for a conſideration, the principle of ſervility and perpetual degradation.

These

Theſe are the ſentiments which we feel to the bottom of our hearts, and we diſcloſe them to the free Parliament of a Monarch whoſe glory it is to reign over a free people.—To you we commit our ſupplications and our cauſe. We have, indeed, little to apprehend, in this benigner age, from the malignant aſperſions of former times, and not more from the obſolete calumnies of former ſtrife; although we ſee them endeavouring again to collect the remnant of their exhauſted venom, before they die for ever, in a laſt and feeble effort to traduce our religion and our principles. But, as oppreſſion is ever fertile in pretexts, we find the objections ſtarted againſt us more dangerous becauſe they are new, or new at leaſt in the novelty of a ſhameleſs avowal. They are principally three —Firſt, it is contended that we are a people originally and fundamentally different from yourſelves, and that our intereſts are for ever irreconcileable, becauſe ſome hundred years ago our anceſtors were conquered by your's. We deny the concluſion; we deny the fact. It is falſe.—In addreſſing ourſelves to you, we ſpeak to the children of our anceſtors, as we alſo are the children of your forefathers: Nature has triumphed over law; we are intermixed in blood; we are blended in connexion; we are one race; we all are Iriſhmen; ſubjects of the Imperial Crown of Ireland. The honour of Parliament is concerned, to repreſs the audacity of thoſe who tell us that you are a foreign colony; and, conſequently, ought to govern according to the principles of invaders, and the policy of recent uſurpation. At leaſt we confide that you will not ſuffer the walls of Parliament to be contaminated with that libel upon the government of Ireland. The ſhaft which was aimed at us has ſtruck yourſelves; a memorable, but, at the ſame time, we truſt, a moſt auſpicious example, to teach both you and us, and our common poſterity, that our intereſts are one; and that whatever affects the well-being and honour of the Roman Catholics, is alſo injurious to the Proteſtant intereſt. Of the ſame complexion and tendency are the two objections,

objections, one that our advancement in property and privilege would lead to a repeal of the act of ſettlement; the other, that our participation in the liberties and franchiſes of our country, would endanger the exiſtence of the conſtitution into which we are admitted.

A reſumption of the lands forfeited by our and your anceſtors, (for they are the ſame), after the lapſe of ſo many years, (near three returns of the longeſt period of legal limitation) after the diſperſion and extinction of ſo many families; after ſo many tranſitions and diviſions, repartitions and reconſolidations of property; ſo many ſales, judgments, mortgages, and ſettlements; and after all the various proceſs of voluntary and legal operation, to conceive the revival of titles dormant for 150 years, is an idea ſo perfectly chimerical, ſo contrary to the experience of all ages and all countries, ſo repugnant to the principles of juriſprudence, and ſo utterly impoſſible in point of fact; that the Roman Catholics of Ireland, once for all, make it their earneſt requeſt to have that queſtion thoroughly inveſtigated, in the aſſured hope, that ſo idle, vain, and abſurb an object of public apprehenſion, being expoſed and laid open to the eye of reaſon, may ſleep in oblivion for ever.

As to the other ſubject of apprehenſion, we have but one anſwer to make. We deſire to partake in the conſtitution; and therefore we do not deſire to deſtroy it. Parliament is now in poſſeſſion of our caſe; our grievances, our ſorrows, our obſtructions, our ſolicitudes, our hopes. We have told you the deſire of our hearts. We do not aſk to be relieved from this or that incapacity; not the abolition of this or that odious diſtinction; not even perhaps to be in the fulneſs of time, and in the accompliſhment of the great comprehenſive ſcheme of legiſlation, finally incorporated with you in the enjoyment of the ſame conſtitution. Even beyond that mark,

we

we have an ultimate and if poffible an object of more interior defire. We look for an union of affections; a gradual, and, therefore, a total obliteration of all the animofities, (on our part they are long extinct), and all the prejudices which have kept us disjoined. We come to you a great acceffion to the Proteftant intereft, with hearts and minds fuitable to fuch an end. We do not come as jealous and fufpicious rivals, to gavel the conftitution, but, with fraternal minds, to participate in the great incorporeal inheritance of freedom, to be held according to the laws and cuftoms of the realm, and by our immediate fealty and allegiance to the King. And fo may you receive us.

And we fhall ever pray.

Objections having been made to this petition, upon Mr. O'Hara's prefenting it, as being informal, he withdrew it; and the general committee finding that fo bold and explicit a ftatement of their cafe had given offence to fome of their more violent opponents, prepared another petition, merely praying that the Houfe would take into confideration, whether the removal of fome of the grievances of the petitioners might not be compatible with Proteftant fecurity. This petition was prefented by Mr. Egan on the 18th of February; and, on the 20th, was afterwards rejected, on a divifion of 200 to 23.

On

On the ſame day was alſo rejected a petition from the Proteſtant inhabitants of Belfaſt, which went much farther than the petition of the Catholics, as it required that they ſhould be placed on the ſame footing with their Proteſtant fellow-ſubjects.

About this time the general committee invited over the ſon of Mr. Burke to act for them as their confidential agent*. They were induced to take this ſtep in order to pay a compliment to Mr. Burke, in return for the extraordinary ſervices he had done for them, and to ſecure, at this juncture, the renewal of his exertions in promoting their cauſe. It was on the 3d January of this year, that Mr. Burke publiſhed his letter to Sir Hercules Langriſhe, in which he gave him that learned and liberal opinion upon the ſubject of the elective franchiſe, which probably obtained the royal aſſent to the meaſure which afterwards was adopted for conceding it. This letter was admirably well adapted to meet every ſpecies of objec-

 tion,

* It appears from the ſtatement, publiſhed by the committee, of the accounts, that they paid Mr. R. Burke for his attendance L.2321, 10s. 5d.

tion, moral, local, and conſtitutional. It was calculated to remove the prejudices of the Church of England, and every ſect of Proteſtant diſſenters; and, above all, it was quite concluſive, as a demonſtration of the compatibility of Catholic emancipation with the coronation oath.

At a meeting of the general committee, on the 4th February, the following reſolutions were agreed to, and afterwards publiſhed, with an addreſs to the Proteſtants, written by Mr. R. Burke, and corrected by his father. To this addreſs were added the anſwers of the foreign Catholic univerſities to queſtions that had been put to them in 1789, at the deſire of Mr. Pitt, concerning the exiſtence and extent of the Popiſh diſpenſing power.

Reſolved, That this committee has been informed, that reports have been circulated, that the application of the Catholics for relief, extends to unlimited and total emancipation; and that attempts have been made, wickedly and falſely, to inſtil into the minds of the Proteſtants of this kingdom an opinion, that our applications were preferred in a tone of menace.

Reſolved, That ſeveral Proteſtant gentlemen have expreſſed great ſatisfaction on being individually informed of the real

extent

extent and respectful manner of the applications for relief, have assured us, that nothing could have excited jealousy, or apparent opposition to us, from our Protestant countrymen, but the above-mentioned misapprehensions.

Resolved, That we therefore deem it necessary to declare, that the whole of our late applications, whether to his Majesty's Ministers, to men in power, or to private members of the legislature, as well as our intended petition, neither did, nor does contain any thing, or extend further, either in substance or in principle, than the four following objects.

1st. Admission to the profession and practice of the law.

2d. Capacity to serve as county magistracies.

3d. A right to be summoned, and to serve on grand and petty juries.

4th. The right of voting in counties only for Protestant members of Parliament; in such a manner, however, as that a Roman Catholic freeholder should not vote, unless he either rented, and cultivated a farm of twenty pounds per annum, in addition to his forty shillings freehold; or else possessed a freehold to the amount of twenty pounds a-year.

Resolved, That, in our opinion, these applications, not extending to any other objects than the above, are moderate, and absolutely necessary for our general alleviation, and more particularly for the protection of the Catholic farmers and the peasantry of Ireland; and that they do not, in any degree, endanger either church or state, or endanger the security of the Protestant interest.

Resolved, That we never had an idea or thought so extravagant, as that of menacing or intimidating our Protestant brethren, much less the legislature; and that we disclaim the violent and turbulent intentions imputed to us in some of the public prints, and circulated in private conversation.

Resolved, That we refer to the known disposition of the Roman Catholics of this kingdom, to our dutiful behaviour, during a long series of years, and particularly to the whole tenor of our late proceedings for the full refutation of every charge of sedition and disloyalty.

Resolved, That for the more ample and detailed exposure of all the evil reports and calumnies circulated against us, an address to our Protestant fellow-subjects, and to the public in general, be printed by the order, and in the name of the general committee.

The queries and answers concerning the Popish dispensing power, are as follow:

1st. Has the Pope or Cardinals, or any body of men, or any individual of the Church of Rome, any civil authority, power, jurisdiction, or pre-eminence whatsoever, within the realm of England?

2d. Can the Pope or Cardinals, or any body of men, or any individual of the Church of Rome, absolve or dispense with his Majesty's subjects from their oath of allegiance, upon any pretext whatsoever?

3d. Is there any principle in the tenets of the Catholic faith, by which Catholics are justified in not keeping faith with

with heretics, or other perſons differing from them in religious opinions, in any tranſaction, either of a public or a private nature?

Abſtract from the Anſwer of the Sacred Faculty of Divinity of Paris to the above Queries.

After an introduction according to the uſual forms of the univerſity, they anſwer the firſt query by declaring:

Neither the *Pope, nor the Cardinals, nor any body of men*, nor any other perſon of the Church of Rome, hath any *civil authority, civil power, civil juriſdiction, or civil pre-eminence* whatſoever in *any* kingdom; and, conſequently, none in the kingdom of England, by reaſon or virtue of any authority, power, juriſdiction, or pre-eminence by divine inſtitution inherent in, or granted, or by any other means belonging to the Pope, or the Church of Rome. This doctrine the Sacred Faculty of Divinity of Paris has always held, and upon every occaſion maintained, and upon every occaſion has rigidly proſcribed the contrary doctrines from her ſchools.

Anſwer to the ſecond query.—Neither the *Pope, nor the Cardinals, nor any body of men*, nor any perſon of the Church of Rome, can, by virtue of the keys, abſolve or releaſe the ſubjects of the King of England from their oath of allegiance.

This and the firſt query are ſo intimately connected, that the anſwer of the firſt immediately and naturally applies to the ſecond, &c.

Anſwer to the third query.—There is no tenet in the Catholic church, by which Catholics are juſtified in not keeping faith with heretics, or thoſe who differ from them in matters

matters of religion. The tenet, that it is lawful to break faith with heretics, is ſo repugnant to common honeſty and the opinions of Catholics, that *there is nothing of which thoſe who have defended the Catholic faith againſt Proteſtants have complained more heavily, than the malice and calumny of their adverſaries in imputing this tenet to them, &c. &c. &c.*

Given at Paris, in the General Aſſembly of the Sorbonne, held on Thurſday the 11th day before the calends of March, 1789.

Signed in due form.

Univerſity of Louvain.

The Faculty of Divinity at Louvain having been requeſted to give her opinion upon the queſtions above ſtated, does it with readineſs—*but ſtruck with aſtoniſhment that ſuch queſtions ſhould, at the end of this eighteenth century, be propoſed to any learned body, by inhabitants of a kingdom that glories in the talents and diſcernment of its natives.* The Faculty being aſſembled for the above purpoſe, it is agreed, with the unanimous aſſent of all voices, to anſwer the firſt and ſecond queries abſolutely in the negative.

The Faculty does not think it incumbent upon her, in this place, to enter upon the proofs of her opinion, or to ſhew how it is ſupported by paſſages in the Holy Scriptures, or the writings of antiquity. That has already been done by Boſſuet, De Marca, the two Barclays, Goldaſtus, the Pithæuſes, Argentre Widrington, and his Majeſty King James the Firſt, in his Diſſertation againſt Bellarmine and Du Perron, and by many others, &c. &c. &c.

The Faculty then proceeds to declare, that the ſovereign power of the ſtate is in nowiſe (not even indirectly, as it is termed

termed) ſubject to, or dependent upon, any other power; though it be a ſpiritual power, or even though it be inſtituted for eternal ſalvation, &c. &c.

That *no man, nor any aſſembly of men,* however eminent in dignity and power, nor even the *whole body of the Catholic church,* though aſſembled in general council, can, upon any ground of pretence whatſoever, weaken the bond of union between the Sovereign and the people; ſtill leſs can they abſolve or free the ſubjects from their oath of allegiance.

Proceeding to the third queſtion, the ſaid Faculty of Divinity *(in perfect wonder that ſuch a queſtion ſhould be propoſed to her)* moſt poſitively and unequivocally anſwers, that there is not, and there never has been, among the Catholics, or in the doctrines of the Church of Rome, any law or principle which makes it lawful for Catholics to break their faith with heretics, or others of a different perſuaſion from themſelves, in matters of religion, either in public or private concerns.

The Faculty declares the doctrine of the Catholics to be, that the divine and natural law, which makes it a duty to keep faith and promiſes, is the ſame; and is neither ſhaken nor diminiſhed, if thoſe, with whom the engagement is made, hold erroneous opinions in matters of religion, &c. &c.

Signed in due form on the 18th of November, 1788.

Univerſity of Valladolid.

To the firſt queſtion it was anſwered—*That neither Pope, Cardinals, or even a General Council,* have any civil authority, power, juriſdiction, or pre-eminence, directly or indirectly, in the kingdom of Great Britain; or over *any other kingdom or province* in which they poſſeſs no temporal dominion.

To

To the ſecond it is anſwered—That neither Pope nor Cardinals, nor even a General Council, can abſolve the ſubjects of Great-Britain from their oaths of allegiance, or diſpenſe with their obligation.

To the third it is anſwered—That the obligation of keeping faith is grounded on the law of nature, which binds all men equally, without reſpect to their religious opinions; and with regard to Catholics, it is ſtill more cogent, as it is confirmed by the principles of their religion.

Signed in the uſual form, February 17, 1789.

While the general committee were occupied in carrying theſe meaſures into effect, Parliament had paſſed a law* for removing part of the reſtraints and diſabilities to which the Catholics were liable. It was introduced into the Houſe of Commons by Sir H. Langriſhe, and, being ſupported by government, it met with little oppoſition. But the conduct of government, on this occaſion, was ſo ſuſpicious, and its favour conferred with ſo bad a grace†, that it did not in the leaſt degree contribute to appeaſe the irritation which its former conduct in 1791 had ſo juſtly given riſe to.

By

* 32d Geo. III. c. 21.

† This meaſure was introduced into the Houſe of Commons without any communication with the general committee.

By this act Catholics may be called to the bar, and may be admitted as students into the King's-Inns. Attornies may take Catholic apprentices, and are relieved from the necessity of educating their children Protestants; and barristers may marry Catholic wives. Catholic barristers, and apprentices to attornies, must, nevertheless, qualify themselves for the benefits of this act, by taking the oath of the 13th and 14th Geo. III. c. 35.

By this act, so much of 9th William III. c. 3. and 2d Anne, c. 6. as prevents Protestants from intermarrying with Papists, is repealed. But Protestants married to Catholics are not to vote at elections; and the law is not altered which makes it a capital felony for a priest to celebrate the marriage of a Protestant and a Catholic, though the very next act in the statute book enables a Presbyterian clergyman to celebrate the marriage of a Protestant and a Presbyterian.

By this act, also, the 7th William III. for restraining foreign education, is repealed; and Catholics are permitted to teach school without taking out a license from the ordinary. And so much likewise of 8th Anne, c. 3. is repealed; which enacts, that no Papist shall take more than two apprentices.

In the course of the debates upon this act, the Catholics were accused of professing tenets inimical to good order, and government; and with harbouring pretensions to the forfeited estates of their forefathers, and with wishing to subvert the existing establishment, that they might reinstate a Popish one in its stead. The general committee were also accused of being turbulent and seditious agitators. It was asserted, that the petition which they presented this year to Parliament was the act of an obscure faction, confined merely to the capital, and disavowed by the great mass of the Catholics.

In order to repel the first of these accusations, the declaration of 1774, which has already been introduced into this work, was republished, and signed by Dr. Troy and the principal Catholic clergy and laity of the kingdom. The second charge was not so easily to be contradicted. It was one of most serious importance to the interests

of

of the whole body, and, if ſuffered to paſs without the fallacy of it being expoſed, would have contributed to defeat all the exertions which had been made to obtain redreſs. Urged by theſe conſiderations, and alſo by a communication, which, about this time, was made, from the firſt authority, that a further application for relief would have great weight with his Majeſty, and with Parliament, if the committee were qualified to declare, that it was the meaſure of every Catholic in the kingdom,* the committee deviſed a plan, by which a convention of delegates ſhould be held, elected by the whole Catholic body. A circular letter was immediately written, directing that each pariſh ſhould proceed to chooſe one or two electors, and that theſe electors ſhould then elect from one to four delegates, as it might appear moſt expedient to them. Their directions were obeyed, and carried into effect with ſo much promptitude and good order, that the convention were able to meet on the 3d of December, without the ſmalleſt degree of tumult or agitation having occurred in any part of the kingdom.

X 2 In

* See the plan for conducting the election of delegates, publiſhed 1793.

In the mean time, this circular letter had been laid hold of by the government as a proper inſtrument with which to rekindle the embers of religious animoſities. Where the partizans of government were ſufficiently ſtrong, corporate and county meetings were held to reprobate the plan of the general committee; but if defeat, or even formidable reſiſtance, was apprehended, ſimilar reſolutions were entered into by the grand juries, where ſucceſs could eaſily be ſecured, from the influence of government in their appointment.

In order to counteract the effect of theſe reſolutions, thoſe Proteſtants who had the virtue and the good ſenſe neither to become the tools or the dupes of government, held a great number of meetings of different towns and diſtricts. Some few, with Londonderry at their head, expreſſed themſelves favourable to a gradual admiſſion of the Catholics; but the great majority followed the example of an immenſe body of volunteers, who, when aſſembled together at their commemoration meeting, declared their ſentiments in favour of the immediate and unqualified exten-

ſion

ſion of the right of ſuffrage to the whole Catholic body.

When the convention met in December, their proceedings were wiſe, temperate, and deciſive, and conducted without any violation of the laws of the land, or of the good order of ſociety. At the firſt meeting the following petition to the King was unanimouſly agreed to, purſuant to inſtructions which had been given to each delegate by his reſpective electors.

To the King's moſt Excellent Majeſty, the humble Petition of the Underſigned Catholics, on behalf of themſelves and the reſt of his Catholic Subjects of the kingdom of Ireland.

Moſt Gracious Sovereign,

We your Majeſty's moſt dutiful and loyal ſubjects of your kingdom of Ireland, profeſſing the Catholic religion, preſume to approach your Majeſty, who are the common father of all your people, and humbly to ſubmit to your conſideration the manifold incapacities and oppreſſive diſqualifications under which we labour.

For, may it pleaſe your Majeſty, after a century of uninterrupted loyalty, in which time five foreign wars and two domeſtic rebellions have occurred, after having taken every oath of allegiance and fidelity to your Majeſty, and given, and being ſtill ready to give, every pledge, which can be deviſed for their peaceable demeanour and unconditional ſubmiſſion

to

to the laws, the Catholics of Ireland ſtand obnoxious to a long catalogue of ſtatutes, inflicting on dutiful and meritorious ſubjects pains and penalties of an extent and ſeverity, which ſcarce any degree of delinquency can warrant, and prolonged to a period, when no neceſſity can be alleged to juſtify their continuance.

In the firſt place, we beg leave, with all humility, to repreſent to your Majeſty, that, notwithſtanding the loweſt departments in your Majeſty's fleets and armies are largely ſupplied by our numbers, and your revenue in this country to a great degree ſupported by our contributions, we are diſabled from ſerving your Majeſty in any office of truſt and emolument whatſoever, civil or military—a proſcription, which diſregards capacity or merit, admits of neither qualification nor degree, and reſts as an univerſal ſtigma of diſtruſt upon the whole body of your Catholic ſubjects.

We are interdicted from all municipal ſtations, and the franchiſe of all guilds and corporations; and our excluſion from the benefits annexed to thoſe ſituations is not an evil terminating in itſelf; for, by giving an advantage over us to thoſe, in whom they are excluſively veſted, they eſtabliſh throughout the kingdom a ſpecies of qualified monopoly, uniformly operating in our disfavour, contrary to the ſpirit, and highly detrimental to the freedom of trade.

We may not found nor endow any univerſity, college, or ſchool, for the education of our children; and we are interdicted from obtaining degrees in the univerſity of Dublin by the ſeveral charters and ſtatutes now in force therein.

We are totally prohibited from keeping or uſing weapons, for the defence of our houſes, families, or perſons, whereby we are expoſed to the violence of burglary, robbery, and aſſaſſination;

aſſaſſination; and to enforce this prohibition, contravening that great original law of nature, which enjoins us to ſelf-defence, a variety of ſtatutes exiſt, not leſs grievous and oppreſſive in their proviſions, than unjuſt in their object; by one of which, enacted ſo lately as within theſe ſixteen years, every one of your Majeſty's Catholic ſubjects, of whatever rank or degree, peer or peaſant, is compellable by any magiſtrate to come forward and convict himſelf of what may be thought a ſingular offence in a country profeſſing to be free—keeping arms for his defence; or, if he ſhall refuſe ſo to do, may incur not only fine and impriſonment, but the vile and ignominious puniſhments of the pillory and whipping, penalties appropriated to the moſt infamous malefactors, and more terrible to a liberal mind than death itſelf.

No Catholic whatſoever, as we apprehend, has his perſonal property ſecure. The law allows and encourages the diſobedient and unnatural child to conform and deprive him of it: the unhappy father does not, even by the ſurrender of his all, purchaſe his repoſe; he may be attacked by new bills, if his future induſtry be ſucceſsful, and again be plundered by due proceſs of law.

We are excluded, or may be excluded, from all petit juries, in civil actions, where one of the parties is a Proteſtant; and we are further excluded from all petit juries in trials by information or indictment founded on any of the Popery laws, by which law we moſt humbly ſubmit to your Majeſty, that your loyal ſubjects, the Catholics of Ireland, are in this their native land, in a worſe ſituation than that of aliens, for they may demand an equitable privilege denied to us, of having half their jury aliens like themſelves.

We may not ſerve on grand juries, unleſs, which it is ſcarcely poſſible can ever happen, there ſhould not be found a ſufficiency

ſufficiency of Proteſtants to complete the pannel; contrary to that humane and equitable principle of the law, which ſays, that no man ſhall be convicted of any capital offence, unleſs by the concurring verdicts of two juries of his neighbours and equals; whereby (and to this, we humbly preſume more particularly to implore your royal attention) we are deprived of the great palladium of the conſtitution, trial by our peers, independent of the manifeſt injuſtice of our property being taxed in aſſeſſments by a body, from which we are formally excluded.

We avoid a further enumeration of inferior grievances; but may it pleaſe your Majeſty, there remains one incapacity, which your loyal ſubjects, the Catholics of Ireland, feel with moſt poignant anguiſh of mind, as being the badge of unmerited diſgrace and ignominy, and the cauſe and bitter aggravation of all our other calamities; we are deprived of the elective franchiſe, to the manifeſt perverſion of the ſpirit of the conſtitution, inaſmuch as your faithful ſubjects are thereby taxed, where they are not repreſented, actually or virtually, and bound by laws, in the framing of which, they have no power to give, or with-hold their aſſent; and we moſt humbly implore your Majeſty to believe, that this our prime and heavy grievance is not an evil merely ſpeculative, but is attended with great diſtreſs to all ranks, and in many inſtances, with the total ruin and deſtruction of the lower orders of your Majeſty's faithful and loyal ſubjects the Catholics of Ireland; for may it pleaſe your Majeſty, not to mention the infinite variety of advantages, in point of protection and otherwiſe, which the enjoyment of the elective franchiſe gives to thoſe who poſſeſs it, nor the conſequent inconveniencies, to which thoſe who are deprived thereof are liable; not to mention the diſgrace to three-fourths of your loyal ſubjects of Ireland, of living the only body of men incapable of franchiſe, in a nation poſſeſſing a free conſtitution, it continually happens, and of neceſſity

necessity from the malignant nature of the law must happen, that multitudes of the Catholic tenantry in divers counties in this kingdom are, at the expiration of their leases, expelled from their tenements and farms to make room for Protestant freeholders, who, by their votes, may contribute to the weight and importance of their landlords; a circumstance which renders the recurrence of a general election, that period which is the boast and laudable triumph of our Protestant brethren, a visitation and heavy curse to us, your Majesty's dutiful and loyal subjects. And may it please your Majesty, this uncertainty of possession to your Majesty's Catholic subjects operates as a perpetual restraint and discouragement on industry and the spirit of cultivation, whereby it happens, that this your Majesty's kingdom of Ireland, possessing many and great natural advantages of soil and climate, so as to be exceeded therein by few, if any countries on the earth, is yet prevented from availing herself thereof so fully as she otherwise might, to the furtherance of your Majesty's honour, and the more effectual support of your service.

And, may it please your Majesty, the evil does not even rest here; for many of your Majesty's Catholic subjects, to preserve their families from total destruction, submit to a nominal confor[illegible]ainst their conviction and their conscience, and preferring perjury to famine, take oaths which they utterly disbelieve; a circumstance, which we doubt not will shock your Majesty's well-known and exemplary piety, not less than the misery which drives those unhappy wretches to so desperate a measure, must distress and wound your royal clemency and commiseration.

And may it please your Majesty, though we might here rest our case on its own merits, justice, and expediency, yet we further presume humbly to submit to your Majesty, that the right of franchise was, with divers other rights, enjoyed by the Catholics of this kingdom, from the first adoption of the English constitution by our forefathers, was secured to at least a great part of our body by the treaty of Limerick, in 1691, guaranteed by your Majesty's royal predecessors, King William and Queen Mary, and finally confirmed and ratified by Parliament; notwithstanding which, and in breach of the public faith of the nation thus solemnly pledged, for which our ancestors paid a valuable consideration, in the surrender of their arms, and a great part of this kingdom, and notwithstanding the most scrupulous adherence, on our part, to the terms of the said treaty, and our unremitting loyalty from that day to the present, the said right of elective franchise was finally and universally taken away from the Catholics of Ireland, so lately as the first year of his Majesty King George the Second.

And when we thus presume to submit this infraction of the treaty of Limerick to your Majesty's royal notice, it is not that we ourselves consider it to be the strong part of our case; for though our rights were recognized, they were by no means created by that treaty; and we do with all humility conceive, that if no such event as the said treaty had ever taken place, your Majesty's Catholic subjects, from their unvarying loyalty, and dutiful submission to the law and from the great support afforded by them to your Majesty's government in this country, as well in their personal service, in your Majesty's fleets and armies, as from the taxes and revenues levied on their property, are fully competent, and justly entitled to participate and enjoy the blessings of the constitution of their country.

And now that we have, with all humility, submitted our grievances to your Majesty, permit us, most gracious Sovereign, again to represent our sincere attachment to the constitution, as established in the three estates of King, Lords, and Commons;

Commons; our uninterrupted loyalty, peaceable demeanour, and ſubmiſſion to the laws for one hundred years; and our determination to perſevere in the ſame dutiful conduct, which has, under your Majeſty's happy auſpices, procured us thoſe relaxations of the penal ſtatutes, which the wiſdom of the legiſlature has from time to time thought proper to grant; we humbly preſume to hope, that your Majeſty, in your paternal goodneſs and affection towards a numerous and oppreſſed body of your loyal ſubjects, may be graciouſly pleaſed to recommend to your Parliament of Ireland, to take into their conſideration the whole of our ſituation, our numbers, our merits, and our ſufferings; and as we do not give place to any of your Majeſty's ſubjects in loyalty and attachment to your ſacred perſon, we cannot ſuppreſs our wiſhes of being reſtored to the rights and privileges of the conſtitution of our country, and thereby becoming more worthy, as well as more capable of rendering your Majeſty that ſervice, which it is not leſs our duty than our inclination to afford.

So may your Majeſty tranſmit to your lateſt poſterity, a crown ſecured by public advantage and public affection; and ſo may your royal perſon become, if poſſible, more dear to your grateful people.

On the 2d January 1793, the gentlemen who had been deputed to preſent this petition were introduced to his Majeſty by Mr. Dundas; and, on the 10th of the ſame month, Lord Weſtmorland, in a ſpeech from the throne to both Houſes of Parliament, ſaid, "I have it in particular com-" mand from his Majeſty to recommend it to " you, to apply yourſelves to the conſideration of

" ſuch meaſures as may be moſt likely to ſtrengthen
" and cement a general union of ſentiment among
" all claſſes of his Majeſty's ſubjects, in ſupport
" of the eſtabliſhed conſtitution; with this view,
" his Majeſty truſts, that the ſituation of his Ma-
" jeſty's Catholic ſubjects will engage your ſerious
" attention; and, in conſideration of this ſub-
" ject, he relies on the wiſdom and liberality of
" Parliament."

In a few days afterwards, Major Hobart, now Lord Buckinghamſhire, preſented to the Houſe of Commons a petition from the Catholics, praying for relief. A petition to the ſame effect was preſented from the Proteſtant inhabitants of Belfaſt, and ſoon after the royal aſſent was given to the following act for affording relief to his Majeſty's Popiſh or Roman Catholic ſubjects of Ireland.

Whereas various acts of Parliament have been paſſed, impoſing on his Majeſty's ſubjects profeſſing the Popiſh or Roman Catholic religion, many reſtraints and diſabilities to which other ſubjects of this realm are not liable; and, from the peaceable and loyal demeanour of his Majeſty's Popiſh or Roman Catholic ſubjects, it is fit that ſuch reſtraints and diſabilities ſhall be diſcontinued: Be it therefore enacted by the King's

King's moſt excellent Majeſty, by and with the advice and conſent of the Lords Spiritual and Temporal, and Commons, in this preſent Parliament aſſembled, and by the authority of the ſame, that his Majeſty's ſubjects being Papiſts, or perſons profeſſing the Popiſh or Roman Catholic religion, or married to Papiſts, or perſons profeſſing the Popiſh or Roman Catholic religion, or educating any of their children in that religion, ſhall not be liable or ſubject to any penalties, forfeitures, diſabilities, or incapacities; or to any laws for the limitation, charging, or diſcovering of their eſtates and property, real or perſonal, or touching the acquiring of property, or ſecurities affecting property, ſave ſuch as his Majeſty's ſubjects of the Proteſtant religion are liable and ſubject to; and that ſuch parts of all oaths as are required to be taken by perſons in order to qualify themſelves for voting at elections of members to ſerve in Parliament; and alſo ſuch parts of all oaths required to be taken by perſons voting at elections for members to ſerve in Parliament, as import to deny that the perſon taking the ſame is a Papiſt, or married to a Papiſt, or educates his children in the Popiſh religion, ſhall not hereafter be required to be taken by any voter, but ſhall be omitted by the perſon adminiſtering the ſame; and that it ſhall not be neceſſary, in order to entitle a Papiſt or perſon profeſſing the Popiſh or Roman Catholic religion to vote at an election of members to ſerve in Parliament, that he ſhould at, or previous to his voting, take the oaths of allegiance and abjuration, any ſtatute now in force to the contrary of any of the ſaid matters in any wiſe notwithſtanding.

2. Provided always, and be it further enacted, That all Papiſts or perſons profeſſing the Popiſh or Roman Catholic religion, who may claim to have a right of voting for members to ſerve in Parliament, or of voting for magiſtrates in any city, town corporate, or borough, within this kingdom, be hereby required to perform all qualifications, regiſtries, and other requiſites,

requisites, which are now required of his Majesty's Protestant subjects in like cases by any law or laws now of force in this kingdom, save and except such oaths and parts of oaths as are herein before excepted.

3. And provided always, That nothing herein before contained shall extend, or be construed to extend to repeal, or alter any law or act of Parliament now in force, by which certain qualifications are required to be performed by persons enjoying any offices or places of trust under his Majesty, his heirs and successors, other than as herein after is enacted.

4. Provided also, That nothing herein contained shall extend or be construed to extend to give Papists or persons professing the Popish religion a right to vote at any parish vestry for levying money to rebuild or repair any parish church, or respecting the demising or disposal of the income of any estate belonging to any church or parish, or for the salary of the parish clerk, or at the election of any church-warden.

5. Provided always, That nothing contained in this act shall extend to or be construed to affect any action or suit now depending, which shall have been brought or instituted previous to commencement of this session of Parliament.

6. Provided also, That nothing herein contained shall extend to authorise any Papist or person professing the Popish or Roman Catholic religion, to have or keep in his hands or possession any arms, armour, ammunition, or any warlike stores, sword-blades, barrels, locks, or stocks of guns or fire-arms, or to exempt such person from any forfeiture or penalty inflicted by any act respecting arms, armour, or ammunition, in the hands or possession of any Papist, or respecting Papists having or keeping such warlike stores, save and except Papists or persons of the Popish or Roman Catholic religion seized of a freehold

a freehold eſtate of one hundred pounds a year, or poſſeſſed of a perſonal eſtate of one thouſand pounds or upwards, who are hereby authoriſed to keep arms and ammunition as Proteſtants now by law may; and alſo ſave and except Papiſts or Roman Catholics poſſeſſing a freehold eſtate of ten pounds yearly value, and leſs than one hundred pounds, or a perſonal eſtate of three hundred pounds, and leſs than one thouſand pounds, who ſhall have at the ſeſſion of the peace in the county in which they reſide taken the oath of allegiance preſcribed to be taken by an act paſſed in the thirteenth and fourteenth years of his preſent Majeſty's reign, entitled, "An Act to "enable his Majeſty's Subjects, of whatever Perſuaſion, to "teſtify their Allegiance to him;" and alſo, in open court, ſwear and ſubſcribe an affidavit that they are poſſeſſed of a freehold eſtate yielding a clear yearly profit to the perſon making the ſame of ten pounds, or a perſonal property of three hundred pounds above his juſt debts, ſpecifying therein the name and nature of ſuch freehold, and nature of ſuch perſonal property; which affidavits ſhall be carefully preſerved by the clerk of the peace, who ſhall have for his trouble a fee of ſix-pence, and no more, for every ſuch affidavit; and the perſon making ſuch affidavits, and poſſeſſing ſuch property, may keep and uſe arms and ammunition as Proteſtants may, ſo long as they ſhall reſpectively poſſeſs a property of the annual value of ten pounds and upwards, if freehold, or the value of three hundred pounds if perſonal, any ſtatute to the contrary notwithſtanding.

7. And be it enacted, That it ſhall and may be lawful for Papiſts or perſons profeſſing the Popiſh or Roman Catholic religion, to hold, exerciſe, and enjoy all civil and military offices, or places of truſt or profit under his Majeſty, his heirs and ſucceſſors, in this kindom; and to hold or take degrees, or any profeſſorſhip in, or be maſters or fellows of any College to be hereafter founded in this kingdom, provided that ſuch

ſuch college ſhall be a member of the univerſity of Dublin, and ſhall not be founded excluſively for the education of Papiſts or perſons profeſſing the Popiſh or Roman Catholic religion, nor conſiſt excluſively of maſters, fellows, or other perſons to be named or elected on the foundation of ſuch college, being perſons profeſſing the Popiſh or Roman Catholic religion, or to hold any office or place of truſt in, and to be a member of any lay body corporate, except the college of the Holy and undivided Trinity of Queen Elizabeth, near Dublin, without taking and ſubſcribing the oath of allegiance, ſupremacy, or abjuration, or making or ſubſcribing the declaration required to be taken, made, and ſubſcribed, to enable any perſon to hold and enjoy any of ſuch places, and without receiving the Sacrament of the Lord's Supper according to the rites and ceremonies of the Church of Ireland, and law, ſtatute, or bye-law of any corporation to the contrary notwithſtanding; provided that every ſuch perſon ſhall take and ſubſcribe the oath appointed by the act, paſſed in the thirteenth and fourteenth years of his Majeſty's reign, entitled, " An Act to " enable his Majeſty's Subjects, of whatever Perſuaſion, to " teſtify their Allegiance to him ;" and alſo the oath and declaration following, that is to ſay :

" I A. B. do hereby declare, that I do profeſs the Roman Catholic religion."

" I A. B. do ſwear, that I do abjure, condemn, and deteſt, as unchriſtian and impious, the principle that it is lawful to murder, deſtroy, or any ways injure any perſon whatſoever for or under the pretence of being a heretic ; and I do declare ſolemnly before God, that I believe, that no act in itſelf unjuſt, immoral, or wicked, can ever be juſtified or excuſed by or under pretence or colour that it was done either for the good of the church, or in obedience to any eccleſiaſtical power whatſoever. I alſo declare, that it is not an article

of

of the Catholic faith, neither am I thereby required to believe or profeſs that the Pope is infallible, or that I am bound to obey any order in its own nature immoral, though the Pope, or any eccleſiaſtical power, ſhould iſſue or direct ſuch order; but, on the contrary, I hold that it would be ſinful in me to pay any reſpect or obedience thereto: I further declare, that I do not believe that any ſin whatſoever committed by me can be forgiven at the mere will of any Pope, or of any prieſt, or of any perſon or perſons whatſoever; but that ſincere ſorrow for paſt ſins, a firm and ſincere reſolution to avoid future guilt, and to atone to God, are previous and indiſpenſible requiſites to eſtabliſh a well-founded expectation of forgiveneſs; and that any perſon who receives abſolution without theſe previous requiſites, ſo far from obtaining thereby any remiſſion of his ſins, incurs the additional guilt of violating a ſacrament; and I do ſwear that I will defend, to the utmoſt of my power, the ſettlement and arrangement of property in this country as eſtabliſhed by the laws now in being; I do hereby diſclaim, diſavow, and ſolemnly abjure any intention to ſubvert the preſent church eſtabliſhment, for the purpoſe of ſubſtituting a Catholic eſtabliſhment in its ſtead; and I do ſolemnly ſwear, that I will not exerciſe any privilege to which I am or may become entitled, to diſturb and weaken the Proteſtant religion and Proteſtant government in this kingdom.

"So help me God."

8. And be it enacted, That Papiſts, or perſons profeſſing the Popiſh or Roman Catholic religion, may be capable of being elected profeſſors of medicine upon the foundation of Sir Patrick Dunne, any law or ſtatute to the contrary notwithſtanding.

9. Provided always, and be it enacted, That nothing herein contained ſhall extend or be conſtrued to extend to enable

any perſon to ſit or vote in either Houſe of Parliament, or to hold, exerciſe, or enjoy the Office of Lord Lieutenant, Lord Deputy, or other Chief Governor or Governors of this kingdom, Lord High Chancellor or Keeper, or Commiſſioner of the Great Seal of this kingdom, Lord High Treaſurer, Chancellor of the Exchequer, Chief Juſtice of the Court of King's Bench or Common Pleas, Lord Chief Baron of the Court of Exchequer, Juſtice of the Court of King's Bench or Common Pleas, or Baron of the Court of Exchequer, Judge of the High Court of Admiralty, Maſter or Keeper of the Rolls, Secretary of State, Keeper of the Privy Seal, Vice-Treaſurer, Teller and Caſhier of the Exchequer, or Auditor General, Lieutenant or Governor, or *Cuſtos Rotulorum* of Counties, Secretary to the Lord Lieutenant, Lord Deputy, or other Chief Governor or Governors of this kingdom, Member of his Majeſty's moſt honourable Privy Council, Prime Serjeant, Attorney-General, Solicitor-General, Second and Third Serjeants at Law, or King's Council, Maſters in Chancery, Provoſt, or Fellow of the College of the holy and undivided Trinity of Queen Elizabeth, near Dublin; Poſt-Maſter General, Maſter and Lieutenant General of his Majeſty's Forces, Generals on the Staff, and Sheriffs, and Sub-ſheriffs of any County in this kingdom; or any office contrary to the rules, orders, and directions made and eſtabliſhed by the Lord Lieutenant and Council, in purſuance of the act paſſed in the ſeventeenth and eighteenth years of the reign of King Charles the Second, entitled, "An Act for the explaining of ſome "Doubts ariſing upon an Act, entitled, An Act for the "better Execution of his Majeſty's gracious Declaration for "the Settlement of his Kingdom of Ireland, and Satisfaction "of the ſeveral Intereſts of Adventurers, Soldiers, and other "his Majeſty's Subjects there, and for making ſome altera- "tions of, and additions unto the ſaid Act, for the more "ſpeedy and effectual Settlement of this Kingdom," unleſs he ſhall have taken, made, and ſubſcribed the oaths and declaration,

claration, and performed the ſeveral requiſites which by any law heretofore made, and now of force, are required to enable any perſon to ſit or vote, or to hold, exerciſe, and enjoy the ſaid offices reſpectively.

10. Provided alſo, and be it enacted, That nothing in this act contained ſhall enable any Papiſt, or perſon profeſſing the Popiſh or Roman Catholic religion, to exerciſe any right of preſentation to any eccleſiaſtical benefice whatſoever.

11. And be it enacted, That no Papiſt, or perſon profeſſing the Popiſh or Roman Catholic religion, ſhall be liable to, or ſubject to any penalty for not attending divine ſervice on the Sabbath-day, called Sunday, in his or her pariſh church.

12. Provided alſo, and be it enacted, That nothing herein contained ſhall be conſtrued to extend to authoriſe any popiſh prieſt, or reputed popiſh prieſt, to celebrate marriage between proteſtant and proteſtant, or between any perſon who hath been, or profeſſed himſelf or herſelf to be a proteſtant at any time within twelve months before ſuch celebration of marriage, and a papiſt, unleſs ſuch proteſtant and papiſt ſhall have been firſt married by a clergyman of the proteſtant religion; and that every popiſh prieſt, or reputed popiſh prieſt, who ſhall celebrate any marriage between two proteſtants, or between any ſuch proteſtant and papiſt, unleſs ſuch proteſtant and papiſt ſhall have been firſt married by a clergyman of the proteſtant religion, ſhall forfeit the ſum of five hundred pounds to his Majeſty, upon conviction thereof.

13. And whereas it may be expedient, in caſe his Majeſty, his heirs and ſucceſſors, ſhall be pleaſed to alter the ſtatutes of the College of the holy and undivided Trinity, near Dublin, and of the univerſity of Dublin, as to enable perſons profeſſing the Roman catholic religion to enter into or to take

z 2 degrees

degrees in the ſaid univerſity, to remove any obſtacle which now exiſts by ſtatute law; be it enacted, That from and after the firſt day of June one thouſand ſeven hundred and ninety-three, it ſhall not be neceſſary for any perſon, upon taking any of the degrees uſually conferred by the ſaid univerſity, to make or ſubſcribe any declaration, or to take any oath, ſave the oaths of allegiance and abjuration, any law or ſtatute to the contrary notwithſtanding.

14. Provided always, That no papiſt or Roman catholic, or perſon profeſſing the Roman catholic or popiſh religion, ſhall take any benefit by or under this act, unleſs he ſhall have firſt taken and ſubſcribed the oath and declaration in this act contained and ſet forth, and alſo the ſaid oath appointed by the ſaid act paſſed in the thirteenth and fourteenth years of his Majeſty's reign, entitled, "An Act to enable his Majeſty's Subjects, of whatever Perſuaſion, to teſtify their Allegiance to him," in ſome one of his Majeſty's four courts in Dublin, or at the general ſeſſions of the peace, or at any adjournment thereof to be holden for the county, city, or borough wherein ſuch papiſt or Roman catholic, or perſon profeſſing the Roman catholic or popiſh religion, doth inhabit or dwell, or before the going judge or judges of aſſize, in the county wherein ſuch papiſt or Roman catholic, or perſon profeſſing the Roman catholic or popiſh religion, doth inhabit and dwell, in open court.

15. Provided always, and be it enacted, That the names of ſuch perſons as ſhall ſo take and ſubſcribe the ſaid oaths and declaration, with their titles and additions, ſhall be entered upon the rolls for that purpoſe to be appointed by ſaid reſpective courts; and that the ſaid rolls, once in every year, ſhall be tranſmitted to, and depoſited in the rolls office in this kingdom, to remain amongſt the records thereof; and the maſters or keepers of the rolls in this kingdom, or their law-

ful

ful deputy or deputies, are hereby empowered and required to give and deliver to ſuch perſon or perſons ſo taking and ſubſcribing the ſaid oaths and declaration, a certificate or certificates of ſuch perſon or perſons having taken and ſubſcribed the ſaid oaths and declaration, for each of which certificates the ſum of one ſhilling and no more ſhall be paid.

16. And be it further provided and enacted, That from and after the firſt day of April one thouſand ſeven hundred and ninety-three, no freeholder, burgeſs, freeman, or inhabitant of this kingdom, being a papiſt or Roman catholic, or perſon profeſſing the Roman catholic or popiſh religion, ſhall at any time be capable of giving his vote for the electing of any knight or knights of any ſhire or county within this kingdom, or citizen or burgeſs to ſerve in any Parliament, until he ſhall have firſt produced and ſhewn to the high ſheriff of the ſaid county, or his deputy or deputies, at any election of a knight or knights of the ſaid ſhire, and to the reſpective chief officer or officers of any city, borough, or town corporate to whom the return of any citizen or burgeſs to ſerve in Parliament, doth or ſhall reſpectively belong, at the election of any citizen or burgeſs to ſerve in Parliament, ſuch certificate of his having taken and ſubſcribed the ſaid oaths and declaration, either from the rolls office, or from the proper officer of the court in which the ſaid oaths and declaration ſhall be taken and ſubſcribed; and ſuch perſon being a freeholder, freeman, burgeſs, or inhabitant, ſo producing and ſhewing ſuch certificate, ſhall be then permitted to vote as amply and fully as any proteſtant freeholder, freeman, burgeſs, or inhabitant of ſuch county, city, borough, or town corporate, but not otherwiſe.*

The

* As no further conceſſions have been made to the Catholics, it may be as well to enumerate here, as in any other place, the various diſabilities to which they are ſtill liable.

Education.—They cannot teach ſchool, unleſs they take the oaths of 13th, 14th Geo III. c. 35. They cannot take Proteſtant ſcholars, or be uſhers to Proteſtant ſchoolmaſters, 32d Geo. III. c. 20.

Guardianſhip.

The general committee, in teſtimony of their gratitude to the King for this moſt important conceſſion, preſented the following addreſs to the Lord

Guardianſhip.—They cannot be guardians, unleſs they take the oaths of 13th, 14th Geo. III. c. 35. If eccleſiaſtics, they cannot, under any circumſtances, be guardians; nor can any Catholic be guardian to a child of a Proteſtant, 30th Geo. III. c. 29.

Marriage.—If a Catholic clergyman marries a Proteſtant and a Catholic, the marriage is null and void, and he is liable to ſuffer death, 32d Geo. III. c. 21.

Self-defence.—No Catholic can keep arms, unleſs he poſſeſſes a freehold eſtate of 10l. per annum, or a perſonal eſtate of 300l. If ſo qualified, he muſt further qualify himſelf by taking the oaths of 13th, 14th Geo. III. c. 35.; unleſs he has a freehold eſtate of 100l per annum, or a perſonal eſtate of 1000l. 33d Geo. III. c. 21.

Exercise of Religion.—The Catholic clergy muſt take the oaths of 13th, 14th Geo. III. c. 35 and regiſter their place of abode, age, and pariſh. No chapel can have a ſteeple or bell, no funeral can take place in any church or chapel-yard, and no rites or ceremonies of the religion or habits of their order are permitted, except within their ſeveral places of worſhip or in private houſes, 21ſt, 22d Geo. III. c. 24. § 6.

Property.—The laws of Anne are in force againſt all Catholics who do not take the oaths of 13th, 14th Geo. III. c. 35.; and alſo againſt all Proteſtants who may have lapſed or become converts to the Catholic religion.

Franchiſes.—No Catholic can hold any of the offices enumerated in § 9. of an act here inſerted.

Catholics cannot ſit in Parliament. They cannot vote at elections for members without taking the oaths of the 13th, 14th Geo. III. c. 35. and of 33d Geo. III. c. 21. They cannot vote at veſtry's. They cannot be barriſters, attorneys, or profeſſors of medicine on Sir P. Dunne's foundation, without taking the oaths of 13th, 14th Geo. III. c. 35 and of 33d Geo. III. c. 21.; or even fowlers and game-keepers.

Catholic Soldiers, by the mutiny act, if they refuſe to frequent the Church of England worſhip, when ordered to do ſo by their commanding officer, ſhall, for the firſt offence, forfeit 2d.; and, for the ſecond, not only forfeit 12d. but be laid in irons for 12 hours; and, by the 2d ſection, art. 5. of the articles of war, the puniſhment even extends to that of death.

An Iriſh Catholic officer or ſoldier on landing in Great Britain, Jerſey, or Guernſey, is immediately liable to the penalty, among others, the Engliſh act 1ſt Geo. I. c. 13 of forfeiting 300l.

Catholics are excluded from holding the offices of Governor, Deputy-Governor or Director of the Bank of Ireland.

No part, ſcarcely, in fact, of the penal code is repealed, but all of it is now the law of the land, and in full force againſt thoſe Catholics who have not qualified themſelves for relief from its violence, by taking the oaths of 13th, 14th Geo. III. c. 35. or who may have lapſed or become converts to the Catholic religion.

Lord Lieutenant, to be by him tranſmitted to his Majeſty.

Moſt Gracious Sovereign,

We your Majeſty's moſt dutiful and loyal ſubjects the Catholics of Ireland, animated with ſentiments of the moſt lively gratitude, beg leave to approach your Majeſty with our ſincere and heartfelt thanks, for the ſubſtantial benefits, which, through your Majeſty's gracious recommendations, we have received from the wiſdom and liberality of Parliament.

Impreſſed with a deep ſenſe of your Majeſty's goodneſs, we reflect, that, in conſequence of this laſt and ſignal inſtance of your royal favour, the diſabilities under which we and our anceſtors ſo long laboured, have, in a conſiderable degree, been removed, the conſtitutional energy of three-fourths of your loyal ſubjects reſtored to their country, and themſelves enabled to teſtify, in a manner more uſeful to your Majeſty's ſervice, their devoted attachment to your perſon, family, and government. Reſtored, as we now are, to ſuch valuable privileges, it ſhall be our duty, as it is our inclination, to unite in ſupport of our excellent conſtitution, as eſtabliſhed in King, Lords, and Commons :—A conſtitution revered by us for its excellence, even when ſecluded from its bleſſings, and from which every advantage we derive becomes a new tie of fidelity and attachment.

Permit us, moſt gracious Sovereign, to expreſs our unfeigned ſatisfaction, that, to a Monarch endeared to us by ſo many proofs of clemency, belongs the glorious diſtinction of being the firſt to begin that work of emancipation, in the accompliſhment of which, we humbly hope, your Majeſty will enjoy the gratification of ſeeing your whole people united in the bonds of equal law and equal liberty.

May

May your Majeſty long continue to reign in the hearts of your faithful ſubjects, diſpenſing, as common father to all your people, the ineſtimable bleſſings of freedom, peace, and union.

The committee likewiſe addreſſed Lord Weſtmoreland! That liberal and conſiſtent Lord Lieutenant, who, in 1790, would not admit the loyal Catholics of Cork *to hope* for any relief from their diſabilities; who, in 1792, ſet on foot the violent reſolutions of the corporations and grand juries againſt all conceſſions to the Catholics; and who, in 1793, was not aſhamed to retrace his ſteps, and become the public organ of his Majeſty's more benevolent and enlightened policy.

Although this act declared that Catholics might hold any military office or employment, as its powers could not extend out of Ireland, and as all Iriſh Catholic ſoldiers, ſailors, and officers, were uniformly employed on ſervices out of Ireland, it was repreſented to the government, that, in order to give it any uſeful effect in this reſpect, the Engliſh act of 1ſt Geo. I. which prohibits Catholics from filling any military ſituation, ſhould be repealed. In anſwer to their application, the Catholics were informed by Lord Hobart, that ſuch a meaſure

measure would be immediately adopted, and the letter of the Secretary of State was shewn to them, containing the promise of the English government. In the House of Lords, when, upon the debate of this act, Lord Farnham proposed an amendment to the clause relating to the military officers, by rendering its operation conditional, until England should pass a similar law, the Chancellor, Lord Clare, opposed it; "for," said he, "it could not "be supposed that his Majesty would appoint a "man to such a post until the laws of the empire "should fully qualify him to act in every part of "it. It was more than probable a similar law to "this would be adopted in England before the "lapse of two months, and, on this ground, the "amendment would be wholly unnecessary."

Fourteen years, however, were allowed to pass by without any such law having been attempted to be adopted in England; and, when the late Ministers sought to rescue the plighted faith of their predecessors from well merited reproach, they were accused of an attempt to subvert the established church, and driven from the councils of his Majesty as the allies of the Pope and the instruments of Bonaparte.

In the course of this year a most unequivocal proof was given of the liberal sentiments which prevailed throughout the Protestants of the North of Ireland, in regard to their Catholic fellow-countrymen. At the meeting of the convention of delegates, which was held in February at Dungannon, and in which the counties of Antrim, Down, Londonderry, Tyrone, Donegal, and Monaghan, were fully represented, they passed resolutions in favour of the absolute necessity of a reform in Parliament, including the unqualified admission of the Catholics. The Synod of Ulster also (a body consisting of the whole dissenting clergy of the North, and the Presbytery of Dublin, together with a lay delegate from each parish) presented an address to the Lord Lieutenant, in which they expressed their satisfaction at the admission of the Catholics to the privileges of the constitution.

These occurrences are of vast importance in forming a correct view of the opinion of the Irish Protestants upon this question; because the Presbyterians being in numbers fully equal to the Protestants of the Church of England, it leaves but

but a ſmall number of the whole people adverſe to the Catholic claims, even if all theſe Proteſtants were, as they certainly are not, hoſtile to emancipation.

During this ſeſſion, another ſubject occupied the ſerious attention of the upper-houſe of Parliament. Diſturbances had broken out, and outrages were committed in the county of Louth, and the neighbouring counties of Meath, Cavan, and Monaghan, by perſons of the very loweſt rank in life, aſſociated under the name of defenders. This body had its origin in religious perſecution, and was an almoſt inevitable conſequence of the ſyſtem, according to which Ulſter had been colonized and ſettled, and Ireland ruled ſince the reformation. In that province Engliſh and Scotch planters had been eſtabliſhed on the forfeited lands of the native Catholics. Theſe laſt were, for the moſt part, obliged to retire to the bogs and mountains; but, even there, they were not permitted to loſe the remembrance of their forefathers, their power and their opulence, in the tranquil enjoyment of ſecurity and content. The bogs and mountains afforded them no refuge againſt the acts of uniformity and ſupremacy, or the accumulating oppreſſions of the Popery laws. Nor were the wretched inhabitants exempted by their defenceleſs condition from the hatred, contempt, and perſecution of their privileged and arrogant neighbours. Hence aroſe a mutual rancorous animoſity between the new ſettlers and natives; or, in other words, between the Proteſtants and Catholics, tranſmitted from generation to generation, until at laſt it became more violent and intolerant than in any other part of Ireland.

The volunteers, by the benign influence of their inſtitution, had, for the firſt time, conſiderably abated this ſpirit; and, by their ſucceſsful activity as military men, in keeping the peace, had prevented its receiving freſh provocation by outrage and inſult. But in proportion as this body declined, or was diſcouraged, prejudices and hatred revived, eſpecially in diſtricts remote from the principal preſbyterian towns, where the growing liberality of the moſt enlightened diſſenters could ſcarcely operate. Theſe prejudices, which chiefly prevailing in the county of Armagh*, extended, leſs

* *Lord Viscount Gosford's Address to the Grand Jury of Armagh.*

Gentlemen—Having requeſted your attendance here this day,

lefs or more, into the adjoining diftricts of the counties of Down and Tyrone, began to break out

day, it becomes my duty to ftate the grounds upon which I thought it advifeable to propofe this meeting, and at the fame time to fubmit to your confideration a plan which occurs to me as moft likely to check the enormities that have already brought difgrace upon this country, and may foon reduce it into deep diftrefs. It is no fecret, that a perfecution, accompanied with all the circumftances of ferocious cruelty, which have in all ages diftinguifhed that dreadful calamity, is now raging in this country. Neither age nor fex, or even acknowledged innocence as to any guilt in the late difturbances, is fufficient to excite mercy, much lefs to afford protection.

The only crime which the wretched objects of this ruthlefs perfecution are charged with, is a crime, indeed, of eafy proof; it is fimply a profeffion of the Roman catholic faith, or an intimate connection with a perfon profeffing this faith. A lawlefs banditti have conftituted themfelves judges of this new fpecies of delinquency, and the fentence they have denounced is equally concife and terrible! It is nothing lefs than a confifcation of all property, and an immediate banifhment. It would be extremely painful, and furely unneceffary, to detail the horrors that attend the execution of fo rude and tremendous profcription—a profcription that certainly exceeds in the comparative number of thofe it configns to ruin and mifery, every example that ancient and modern hiftory can fupply: for, where have we heard, or in what ftory of human cruelties have we read of more than half the inhabitants of a populous country deprived at one blow of the means as well as of the fruits of their induftry, and driven, in the midft of an inclement feafon, to feek a fhelter for themfelves and

out in the year 1791. About that period ſeveral aſſociations, among the lower orders of the Proteſtants,

and their helpleſs families where chance may guide them. This is no exaggerated picture of the horrid ſcenes now acting in this county. Yet ſurely it is ſufficient to awaken ſentiments of indignation and compaſſion in the coldeſt boſoms. Theſe horrors are now acting with impunity. The ſpirit of impartial juſtice (without which law is nothing better than an inſtrument of tyranny) has for a time diſappeared in this county, and the ſupineneſs of the magiſtracy of Armagh is become a common topic of converſation in every corner of the kingdom.

It is ſaid in reply, the catholics are dangerous; they may be ſo—they may be dangerous from their numbers, and ſtill more dangerous from the unbounded views they have been encouraged to entertain; but I will venture to aſſert, without fear of contradiction, that theſe proceedings are not more contrary to humanity than they are to ſound policy. It is to be lamented, that no civil magiſtrate happened to be preſent with the military detachment on the night of the 21ſt inſtant; but, I truſt, the ſuddenneſs of the occaſion, the unexpected and inſtantaneous aggreſſion on the part of the delinquents, will be univerſally admitted as a full vindication of the conduct of the officer, and the party acting under his command. Gentlemen, I have the honour to hold a ſituation in this county, which calls upon me to deliver my ſentiments, and I do it without fear and without diſguiſe. I am as true a proteſtant as any gentleman in this room, I inherit a property which my family derived under a proteſtant title, and, with the bleſſing of God, I will maintain that title to the utmoſt of my power. I will never conſent to make a ſacrifice of proteſtant

teſtants, were formed, under the appellation of *Peep-a-day Boys*, whoſe object was to ſcour the

Catholic

proteſtant aſcendancy to catholic claims, with whatever menace they may be urged, or however ſpeciouſly or invidiouſly ſupported. Conſcious of my ſincerity in this public declaration, which I do not make unadviſedly, but as the reſult of mature deliberation, I defy the paltry inſinuations that malice or party-ſpirit may ſuggeſt.

I know my own heart, and I ſhould deſpiſe myſelf, if, under any intimidation, I could cloſe my eyes againſt ſuch ſcenes as preſent themſelves on every ſide, or my ears againſt the complaints of a perſecuted people.

I ſhould be guilty of an unpardonable injuſtice to the feelings of gentlemen here preſent, were I to ſay more on this ſubject. I have now acquitted myſelf to my conſcience and my country, and take the liberty of propoſing the following reſolutions:

1ſt. That it appears to this meeting, that the county of Armagh is at this moment in a ſtate of uncommon diſorder; that the Roman catholic inhabitants are grievouſly oppreſſed by lawleſs perſons unknown, who attack and plunder their houſes by night, and threaten them with inſtant deſtruction, unleſs they immediately abandon their lands and habitations.

2d. That a committee of magiſtrates be appointed to ſit on Tueſdays and Saturdays in the chapter-room in the town of Armagh, to receive information againſt all perſons of whatever deſcription, who diſturb the peace of this county.

3d.

Catholic diſtricts about the break of day, and ſtrip the inhabitants of fire-arms, alledging that they were warranted in ſo doing by the Popery laws, which had indeed for a long period forbidden, to the members of that communion, the uſe of arms, even for ſelf-defence.

The Catholics, thus expoſed and attacked, entered into a counter-aſſociation called defenders, which derived its name from the neceſſity of their ſituation,

3d. That the inſtruction of the whole body of magiſtrates to their committee ſhall be to uſe every legal means within their power to ſtop the progreſs of the perſecution now carrying on by an ungovernable mob againſt the Roman catholic inhabitants of this county.

4th. That ſaid committee, or any three of them, be empowered to expend any ſum or ſums of money, for information or ſecret ſervice, out of the fund ſubſcribed by the gentlemen of this county.

5th. That a meeting of the whole body of the magiſtracy be held every ſecond Monday, at the houſe of Mr. Charles M'Reynolds, in the town of Armagh, to hear the reports of the committee, and to give ſuch further inſtructions as the exigence of the caſe may require.

6th. That offenders of every deſcription in the preſent diſturbances ſhall be proſecuted out of the fund ſubſcribed by the gentlemen of this county.

ſituation, and its excuſe from the difficulty, or as they ſtated, the impoſſibility of obtaining juſtice againſt their aggreſſors. This aſſociation, at firſt local and confined, as much as mutual hatred would allow, to actual ſelf-defence, began in 1792 to ſpread through other parts of the kingdom, and not a little to connect itſelf with more general politics.

In proportion as this aſſociation extended itſelf into diſtricts where no Proteſtants of inferior rank in life were to be found, and therefore no outrages like thoſe committed by the *Peep-a-day Boys* to be apprehended, it gradually loſt its characteriſtic of being a religious feud, and became, in fact, an aſſociation of the very loweſt orders, particularly for procuring a redreſs of the grievances of the very loweſt orders. Even in the counties where it originated, it ceaſed to be actuated by religious animoſity before the end of 1792, in conſequence of the exertions of the early United Iriſhmen, whoſe chief endeavours were always directed to reconcile the Proteſtants and Catholics*.

* This very accurate account of the origin and progreſs of the defenders is taken from a late publication in America.

Theſe diſturbances having attracted the attention of the Houſe of Lords early in 1793, a ſecret committee was appointed to inquire into their cauſes, to endeavour to diſcover their promoters, and to prevent their extenſion.

In their report they exculpate the Catholics as a body from all criminality with reſpect to theſe proceedings. They ſay, " That nothing appeared " before them which could lead them to believe " that the body of the Roman Catholics in this " kingdom were concerned in promoting or coun- " tenancing ſuch diſturbances;" and then they even acquit the lower orders of Catholics of being to blame, by ſaying, " That if all the Magiſtrates " in the diſturbed counties had followed the " ſpirited example of the few, who, much to their " honour, exerted themſelves with vigour and " courage to ſupport the laws, the committee are " perſuaded, that theſe diſturbances might have " been ſuppreſſed; but, inſtead of doing ſo, they " remained inactive."

In further corroboration of the innocence of the Catholics, there is the following declaration of one

one of the members of the committee in the debate on the Catholic bill. Lord Portarlington ſaid, "That if he was not fully convinced that "the Catholic body had no connection whatever "in the diſturbances created by ſome of their "communion in the North, he ſhould never give "this bill his ſupport."

The Catholic clergy, who have been uniformly ready to promote tranquillity, and inculcate the obligation of a ſtrict ſubmiſſion to the laws, were not backward, on this occaſion, in aſſiſting government to ſuppreſs the outrages of the defenders. Dr. Troy, Dr. O'Reilly, Dr. Bray, Dr. Bellew, and Dr. Cruiſe, all of them titular biſhops, happening to be in Dublin when the buſineſs was firſt taken up to the Houſe of Lords, publiſhed the following admonition to thoſe of their communion, and directed the prieſts of their dioceſes to read it in their reſpective chapels.

Dear Chriſtians, Dublin, January 25, 1793.

It has been our conſtant practice, as it is our indiſpenſable duty, to exhort you to manifeſt on all occaſions, that unſhaken loyalty to his Majeſty, and obedience to the laws, which the principles of our holy religion inſpire and command. This loyalty and obedience have ever peculiarly diſtinguiſhed the Roman Catholics of Ireland. We do not conceive a doubt of their being actuated at present by the same sentiments; but think it necessary to observe, that a most lively gratitude to our beloved Sovereign should render their loyalty and love of order, if possible, more conspicuous. Our gracious King, the common father of all his people, has, with peculiar energy, recommended his faithful Roman Catholic subjects of this kingdom to the wisdom and liberality of our enlightened Parliament. How can we, dear Christians, express our heartfelt acknowledgment for this signal and unprecedented instance of royal benevolence and condescension! Words are insufficient; but your continued and peaceable conduct will more effectually proclaim them, and in a manner equally, if not more satisfactory and pleasing to his Majesty and his Parliament. Avoid then, we conjure you, dearest brethren, every appearance of riot: attend to your industrious pursuits for the support and comfort of your families; fly from idle assemblies; abstain from the intemperate use of spirituous and intoxicating liquors; practise the duties of our holy religion: this conduct, so pleasing to Heaven, will also prove the most powerful recommendation of your present claims to our amiable Sovereign, to both Houses of Parliament, to the magistrates, and to all our well meaning fellow-subjects of every description. None but the evil-minded can rejoice in your being concerned in any disturbance.

We cannot but declare our utmost and conscientious detestation and abhorrence of the enormities lately committed by seditious and misguided wretches of every religious denomination, in some counties of this kingdom; they are enemies to God and man, the outcasts of society, and a disgrace to Christianity: we consider the Roman Catholics amongst them unworthy the appellation; whether acting from themselves, or seduced to outrage by arts of designing enemies to us, and to national prosperity, intimately connected with our emancipation.

Offer

Offer your prayers, dearest brethren, to the Father of mercy, that he may inspire these deluded people with sentiments becoming Christians and good subjects; supplicate the Almighty Ruler and Disposer of empires, by whom kings rule and legislators determine what is just, to direct his Majesty's councils, and forward his benevolent intentions to unite all his Irish subjects in bonds of common interest, and common endeavours for the preservation of peace and good order, and for every purpose tending to encrease and secure national prosperity.

Beseech the throne of Mercy also, to assist both Houses of Parliament in their important deliberations; that they may be distinguished by consummate wisdom and liberality, for the advantage of the kingdom, and the relief and happiness of his Majesty's subjects.

Under the pleasing expectations of your cheerful compliance with these our earnest solicitations, we most sincerely wish you every blessing in this life, and everlasting happiness in the next; through our Lord Jesus Christ. Amen.

At the close of the sessions of Parliament, Lord Westmorland began his speech from the throne with these words, "The wisdom and liberality "with which you attended to his Majesty's royal "recommendation in favour of his Roman Catho-"lic subjects, are highly pleasing to the King." Did, then, Mr. Pitt put into the mouth of the Viceroy what was not true; or does his Majesty not consider that policy to be wise and liberal in

1808,

1808, which he thought so wise and liberal in 1793? It will be well for those who run away with an opinion, that the King is and always has been severely adverse to concessions to the Catholics of Ireland, to examine the various documents of this kind which are to be found in the history of the concessions which have been made during his reign. Let them compare the opinions contained in these documents with those which are now imputed to his Majesty; and let them compare the concessions which have been granted with those which remain to be granted, and the conclusion which they must draw from such a comparison is this, that it is absolutely impossible that there can be any foundation whatever for those assertions which have been of late so loudly re-echoed from one end of the empire to the other, that his Majesty entertains a conscientious objection to the complete emancipation of the Catholics. But to say, that it is impossible to believe them, is to say but little; it amounts to no less than a libel upon his Majesty's character to maintain doctrines so entirely irreconcileable with the whole tenor of his reign.

In

In the summer of 1794, Mr. Pitt formed his memorable coalition with the Rockingham party; and though the ground of this transaction was a concurrence of opinion concerning the war with France, "if the general management and super-"intendance of Ireland had not been offered to "the Duke of Portland, that coalition could "never have taken place: The sentiments that "he had entertained, and the language he had "held so publicly for years back on the subject, "rendered the superintendance of Irish affairs a "point that could not be dispensed with by "him."* It having thus become a point that could not be dispensed with by the Duke of Portland† to grant the Catholics of Ireland complete emancipation, the first measure of his Grace, immediately upon the coalition being arranged, was to solicit Lord Fitzwilliam to accept of the office of Lord Lieutenant, and to propose to him to carry this measure instantly into effect.‡ This measure was decided upon by the Cabinet on the

day

* Letter from Lord Fitzwilliam to Lord Carlisle.

† The reader may possibly suppose that this Duke of Portland is not the Duke of Portland now at the head of the present Administration. He may, however, rely upon it, that the fact is so.

‡ Lord Fitzwilliam's letter to Lord Carlisle.

day the Duke of Portland kiſſed hands, after frequent conſultations between Mr. Pitt, the Duke of Portland, Lord Fitzwilliam, Mr. Grattan, and Mr. Ponſonby.*

Lord Fitzwilliam having acceded to the preſſing ſolicitations of the Duke of Portland, to undertake to carry this favourite and indiſpenſable meaſure into effect, landed in Dublin on the 2d of January. He had conſented not to bring the queſtion forward on the part of government, but rather to endeavour to keep it back until a period of more general tranquillity; "*but it had been reſolved by* "*the Cabinet, that, if the Catholics ſhould appear* "*determined to ſtir the buſineſs, and bring it be*-"*fore Parliament, then he was to give it a hand*-"*ſome ſupport on the part of government.*"† But no ſooner was Lord Fitzwilliam landed than he found this determination had been taken by the Catholics.

The Catholics of Dublin had held a meeting on the 23d of December, and agreed to a petition to Parliament, claiming the repeal of all the penal laws. Similar petitions had been agreed to throughout

* Lord Fitzwilliam's letter to Lord Carliſle. † Ibid.

throughout the whole kingdom, the natural consequences of its being known for ſome months, that ſo ſteady and ſtrenuous a friend to emancipation as the Duke of Portland had become one of his Majeſty's Miniſters. Lord Fitzwilliam finding, therefore, that the queſtion would force itſelf upon his immediate conſideration, communicated his opinion and intentions to the Engliſh government, on the third day after his arrival, in the following terms: "That, not to grant chearfully, on the part of government, all the Catholics wiſhed for, would not only be exceedingly impolitic, but perhaps dangerous; that in doing this no time was to be loſt; that the buſineſs would preſently be at hand; and that, *if he received no very peremptory directions to the contrary*, he would acquieſce to the wiſhes of the Catholics."*

Parliament met on the 22d of January, and on the 12th of February, "no peremptory directions to the contrary having arrived," though ſo much time had elapſed ſince Lord Fitzwilliam had communicated his intentions to the Engliſh government, Mr. Grattan, with the conſent of

* Lord Fitzwilliam's letter to Lord Carliſle.

Lord Fitzwilliam, moved for leave to bring in a bill for the farther relief of the Catholics.

Meanwhile the English Cabinet forgot the stipulations which they had entered into with Lord Fitzwilliam, "*that if the Catholics should* "*appear determined to stir the business and bring* "*it before Parliament, he was to give it a hand-* "*some support on the part of government*," and the Duke of Portland was directed by Mr. Pitt to inform Lord Fitzwilliam, that, notwithstanding the length to which the Irish government had gone, it must retrace its steps. "Then," says Lord Fitzwilliam in his letter to Lord Carlisle, "it appears to have been discovered that "the deferring of it would be not merely an ex-"pediency or thing to be desired for the present, "but the means of doing a greater good to the "British empire, than it has been capable of re-"ceiving since the revolution, *or at least since the* "*union*."

Lord Fitzwilliam having refused to become an accomplice in the tergiversation of Mr. Pitt and the Duke of Portland, that fatal measure of his

recal

recal was determined upon ; a meaſure which has involved Ireland in 13 years of ſuffering under military tyranny, inſurrection, and rebellion, and which at length has ſhook the ſtability of the empire to its centre.

Upon a debate in the Houſe of Lords, which took place ſoon after Lord Fitzwilliam's return to England, on the ſubject of his conduct in Ireland, Lord Weſtmorland ſaid, by the directions of Mr. Pitt, "That he had no authority whatever from Miniſters in this country for taking the ſteps which he had done on the Catholic queſtion." The incorrectneſs, however, of this aſſertion, it is now no very difficult matter to expoſe. In the firſt place, the meaſure of emancipation to the Catholics was originally the meaſure of Mr. Pitt and the Weſtmorland adminiſtration.* "The moſt ſtrenuous and zealous friends," ſays Lord Fitzwilliam, "of my predeceſſor, claimed the credit of it for their patron in terms of the higheſt compliment. They did it in the Houſe of Commons, they did it in the Houſe of Lords laſt night. The perſons whom Lord Weſtmor-

* Lord Fitzwilliam to Lord Carliſle.

"land then principally consulted, opposed it, but "the open interference of Lord Hobart, the "avowed determination of the British Cabinet, "communicated as such to the Catholic agents "on the spot, as through the medium of confi- "dential persons sent over to England for that "purpose, bore down the opposition. The decla- "rations of Mr. Pitt and Mr. Dundas are well "known in this country, and are often quoted. "They would not risk a rebellion in Ireland on "such a question."

Here then is evidence, which has never been disputed, that, even before Lord Fitzwilliam went to Ireland, the measure had been determined upon by Mr. Pitt. The only question, therefore, to be decided, in judging of the truth of Lord Westmorland's assertion, is, whether or not Mr. Pitt had consented that the proper time for adopting this measure was arrived, when Lord Fitzwilliam was sent to Ireland. That he had so consented there is in proof "the language which the Duke "of Portland had held so publicly for years "back," that the emancipation of the Catholics was indispensably necessary. There is the fact of

his

his refufing to coalefce with Mr. Pitt, unlefs this meafure was conceded; there are the frequent confultations that took place concerning it between Mr. Pitt, Lord Fitzwilliam, Mr. Grattan, and Mr. Ponfonby; the acceptance alfo of the office of Lord Lieutenant by Lord Fitzwilliam; and, finally, the word and honour of Lord Fitzwilliam, that his confent was abfolutely given. All thefe circumftances there are in direct contradiction of the affertion of Lord Weftmoreland. But befides all thefe occurrences, there is the remarkable fentence in the Duke of Portland's difpatch, that the deferring of the meafure would be "the means of doing a greater good to "the Britifh Empire, than it had been capable of "receiving fince the revolution, *or at leaft fince* "*the union.*" This fhews that it was the object of Mr. Pitt's mind, at that time, to carry the union, and fully accounts for Mr. Pitt's perfidy and the recal of Lord Fitzwilliam. All the events which have fince taken place concerning the union, are evidence in favour of Lord Fitzwilliam's integrity and Mr. Pitt's duplicity; they are conclufively contradictory of the affertion of Lord Weftmoreland, and fully expofe one of the moſt flagitious tranſactions that the annals of hiſtory have recorded in the worſt of times, and by the baſeſt of governments.

When the differences that exiſted between the Lord Lieutenant and the Engliſh Cabinet were known, grief and conſternation ſeized all who had flattered themſelves that the meaſures of his Excellency's adminiſtration were to redreſs the grievances, remove the diſcontents, and work the ſalvation of Ireland. In the Houſe of Commons, Sir Lawrence Parſons moved to limit the money bills to two months; but Lord Milton and Mr. George Ponſonby deprecated the meaſure, and it was rejected. The Houſe of Commons, however, unanimouſly reſolved, that his Excellency had, by his conduct ſince his arrival, merited the thanks of the Houſe, and the confidence of the people.

Out of Parliament the diſcontent was more manifeſt. The Catholics, who had now for ſix months felt ſecure of being at length relieved from the execrable ſyſtem of pains and penalties, as the Duke of Portland himſelf was accuſtomed to call it, now ſaw the cup daſhed from their lips, and could

could not but despair of ever seeing a termination to the perfidy of the English Cabinets. Those of Dublin, impelled by these feelings, assembled on the 27th of February, and voted a petition to the King for the continuance of Lord Fitzwilliam as their Chief Governor; and the Catholics of the whole kingdom followed their example, by adopting resolutions and addresses expressive of the same sentiments.

The Protestants, too, assembled extensively, and as loudly spoke their indignation at what they condemned as ministerial treachery, and considered as a great public calamity. The freemen and freeholders of the city of Dublin, like the Catholics, agreed to a petition to the King. The merchants and traders of the city expressed their sorrow at the rumoured recal of his Excellency, and their entire concurrence in the removal of all religious disabilities. The counties of Kildare, Wexford, Antrim, and Londonderry, followed the example of the freemen and freeholders of the capital, and the same sentiments seemed to pervade every part of the kingdom. The active republicans and new united Irishmen alone were not

sorry

ſorry at the agitation and controverſies which were now ſpringing up.

These expreſſions, however, of diſſatisfaction on the part of the Iriſh people, were of no avail. A ſyſtem of burning and torture was to ſucceed a ſyſtem of conciliation, for the purpoſe of preparing Ireland for the union, and Lord Camden was, accordingly, ſelected as a fit perſon to ſucceed Lord Fitzwilliam as Lord Lieutenant.

The meaſure of union comes the next in the courſe of the events in which the Catholics as a body were concerned; and, in ſtrict propriety, it would be right now to proceed to ſhew how the Catholics were affected by it. But as there have been, and ſtill are, thoſe who, either through ignorance or in defiance of all regard for truth, aſſert that the rebellion of 1798 was a Catholic rebellion, and that the conduct of the Catholics on that occaſion affords a juſtification for refuſing to grant them further conceſſions, it will contribute to promote a more juſt view of the ſubject, if thoſe facts are referred to, which exiſt, in refutation of the ſuppoſition that the Catholics, as a body, were concerned in this rebellion.

Fortunately

Fortunately for the cauſe of truth and juſtice, there do exiſt documents, the authority of which no ſophiſtry or calumny can impeach. Theſe are the reports of the Committees of the Iriſh Parliament. They ſo minutely explain the cauſe, the conduct, and the character of this rebellion, and give ſuch accurate information reſpecting thoſe who were concerned in it, that it is impoſſible for any one to affix to it any other character than that which they have given to it. The juſtification, therefore, of the Catholics, by theſe reports, reſts upon this circumſtance, that, to maintain that the rebellion was a Catholic rebellion, is to diſpute the authority of theſe reports, which make no ſuch charge, and account for it by other means.

The following extracts from the report of the Committee of the Houſe of Commons, appointed, in 1798, to examine the evidence, contains a faithful deſcription of the origin and object of this tranſaction.

" The ſociety under the name of United Iriſhmen, it appears, was eſtabliſhed in 1791; its founders held forth what they termed Catholic emancipation and parliamentary reform, as the oftenfible objects of their union: but it clearly appeared, from the letter of Theobald Wolfe Tone, accompanying their original conftitution, as tranfmitted to Belfaft for their adoption, that, from its commencement, the real purpofe of thofe who were at the head of the inftitution, was to feparate Ireland from Great Britain, and to fubvert the eftablifhed conftitution of this kingdom: in corroboration of which, your committee have annexed to this report feveral of their early publications, particularly a profpectus of the fociety which appeared in the beginning of the year 1791; as alfo the plan of reform they recommended to the people."

"For the firft three years their attention was entirely directed to the engaging in their fociety perfons of activity and talents, in every quarter of the kingdom; and in preparing the public mind for their future purpofes, by the circulation of the moft feditious publications, particularly the works of Mr. Thomas Paine. At this time, however, the leaders were rather cautious of alarming minds not fufficiently ripe for the adoption of

their

their principles, by the too open diſcloſure of the real objects which they had in view. In 1795, the teſt of the ſociety underwent a ſtriking reviſion; the words in the amended teſt ſtand, "a "full repreſentation of the people," omitting the words, "in the Commons Houſe of Parliament;" the reaſon for which has been admited by three members of the executive, examined before your committee, to be the better to reconcile reformers and republicans in a common exertion to overthrow the ſtate."

"In the ſummer of 1796, great numbers of perſons, principally in the province of Ulſter, had enrolled themſelves in this ſociety. About the ſame period, as will be more fully explained hereafter, a direct communication had been opened by the heads of the party with the enemy, and French aſſiſtance was ſolicited and promiſed to be ſpeedily ſent to aid the diſaffected in this kingdom."

"With a view of being prepared as much as poſſible to co-operate with the enemy then expected, and in order to counteract the effect of the armed aſſociations of yeomanry eſtabliſhed in October 1796, directions were iſſued by the leaders to the ſocieties to form themſelves into military bodies, and to be provided with arms and ammunition."

"These directions were ſpeedily obeyed; the ſocieties aſſumed a new military form; and, it appears by the original papers ſeized at Belfaſt in the month of April 1797, that their numbers, at that period, in the province of Ulſter alone, were ſtated to amount to nearly 100,000 men. That they were very largely ſupplied with fire-arms and pikes; that they had ſome cannon and ammunition, and were diligently employed in the ſtudy of military tactics; in ſhort, that nothing was neglected by the party which could enable them to take the field on the arrival of the enemy, or whenever they might receive orders to that effect from their ſuperior officers, whom they were bound by oath to obey."

In the report of the committee of 1797, it appears that no part of the kingdom, in which the Catholic population prevails, was organized, except the counties of Weſt Meath, and Kildare, and the city of Dublin.

These extracts establish the following facts. 1st. That the persons who were the founders of the rebellion were those who formed the first societies of United Irishmen, who were all Protestants.

2d. That the object of the rebellion was a republican form of government, and separation from England, and not Catholic emancipation, or the establishment of the Catholic religion.

3d. That, in May 1797, the province of Ulster being inhabited almost entirely by Protestants, no Catholics whatever were concerned, except some of the lowest orders in Dublin, and in the counties of Westmeath and Kildare; and,

4th. That 100,000 Protestants were, in May 1797, completely organized for open rebellion, and well supplied with arms.

Now, as we learn from the evidence of Mr. M'Nevin before the committee of the House of Lords in 1798, that the leaders of the treason had been determined to commence operations

in

in 1797, let us ſuppoſe the rebellion had then broke out, and aſk this queſtion, Would it have been a Catholic rebellion? Certainly not. No man could venture to maintain an opinion ſo utterly untenable. Then, if the rebellion, if it had broken out in 1797, would have been a rebellion of Proteſtants, and not one of Catholics, how could it become a Catholic rebellion in 1798? Let us again refer to the report of the ſecret committee. This gives an accurate account of the progreſs of the rebellion during the year 1797, and ſhews by what means, and *by whom*, the deluded Catholic peaſantry of the South were made parties to the treaſon.

"It appears to your committee, that the leaders of the treaſon, apprehenſive leſt the enemy might be diſcouraged from any further plan of invaſion, by the loyal diſpoſition manifeſted throughout Munſter and Connaught on their former attempt, (by Hoche in December 1796), determined to direct all their exertions to the propagation of the ſyſtem in thoſe provinces, which had hitherto been but partially infected. With this view emiſſaries were ſent into the South and Weſt in great numbers,

numbers, of whofe fuccefs in forming new focieties, and adminiftering the oaths of the union, there were, in the courfe of a few months, but too evident proofs, in the introduction of the fame difturbances and enormities into Munfter, with which the northern province had been fo feverely vifited."

"In order to engage the peafantry in the fouthern counties, particularly in the counties of Waterford and Cork, the more eagerly to their caufe, the United Irifhmen found it expedient, in urging their general principles, to dwell with peculiar energy on the fuppofed oppreffivenefs of tythes (which had been the pretext for the old Whiteboy infurrections); and it is obfervable, that, in addition to the acts of violence ufually reforted to by the party, for the furtherance of their purpofes, the ancient practice of burning the corn, and houghing the cattle of thofe againft whom their refentment was directed, was revived, and very generally practifed in thofe counties."

"With a view to excite the refentment of the Catholics, and to turn their refentment to the

purpofes

purposes of the party, fabricated and false tests were presented as having been taken to exterminate Catholics; and were industriously disseminated by the emissaries of the treason throughout the provinces of Leinster, Munster, and Connaught. Reports were frequently circulated amongst the ignorant of the Catholic persuasion, that large bodies of men were coming to put them to death. This fabrication, however extravagant, was one among the many wicked means by which the deluded peasantry were engaged the more readily in the treason."

"The measures thus adopted by the party completely succeeded in detaching the minds of the lower classes from their usual habits and pursuits; insomuch, that, in the course of the autumn and winter 1797, the peasantry in the midland and southern counties were sworn and ripe for insurrection."

From this account of the progress of the treason in 1797, in the south of Ireland, the following inferences may be deduced:—1st. That the Catholics of Ireland were unconnected with the

system

ſyſtem of rebellion which had extended over the whole of the Proteſtant province of Ulſter; 2d. That the peaſantry of the ſouth were corrupted by emiſſaries ſent amongſt them by the leaders of the treaſon in the north, and not by the Catholic clergy or Catholic ariſtocracy; and, 3d. That the organization of the ſouth was not a diſtinct effort of a diſtinct body of people, but a meaſure ſubſidiary to the original organization of the Proteſtants of the north, conducted by the ſame party, and having the ſame object in contemplation.

Then it follows, that the leaders of the rebellion being the ſame in 1798 as they were in 1797; the object of it the ſame in 1798 as it was in 1797; the means for carrying it into effect in 1798 the ſame as the means for carrying it into effect in 1797; there can be no more grounds for calling it a Catholic rebellion in 1798, than there were for calling it a Catholic rebellion in 1797; and, therefore, as there were no grounds for affixing this character to it in 1797, neither were there any for calling it a Catholic rebellion in 1798.

In direct contradiction, however, of such a conclusion, and of the statements of the secret committee, it has been asserted by those who are interested in calumniating the Catholic character, and believed by those who are ignorant of its true nature, that the rebellion of Ireland was a Catholic rebellion; that the designs of the Catholic body went to the massacre and destruction of every Protestant in Ireland; and that all their other plans were wholly subservient to that of establishing the Catholic religion.*

As

* These are the propositions which Sir Richard Musgrave has laboured to maintain. His work professes to do that which the secret committee of the House of Commons was appointed to do, namely, to give a faithful account of this rebellion. A discerning public will at once see to which authority they ought to give a preference. Sir Richard dedicated his first edition to Lord Cornwallis. Upon reading it, however, Lord Cornwallis directed his Secretary to write the following letter to him:

SIR, *Dublin, March* 24, 1801.

I am directed by the Lord Lieutenant to express to you his concern at its appearing, that your late publication of the history of the Rebellions of Ireland has been dedicated to him by permission. Had his Excellency been apprized of the contents and nature of the work, he would never have lent the sanction of his name to a book which tends so strongly to revive the dreadful animosities which have so long distracted this country, and which it is the duty of every good subject

As to the conduct of the Catholic clergy of the county of Wexford, it is now well known, "that "not one of them who had a flock, not one parish "priest was implicated, or had any concern in "fomenting, encouraging, or aiding the rebellion; "nay, it is certain, that they abhorred, and detested, and shuddered at it, as the most wicked, "scandalous, and abominable event that they had "ever witnessed."*

The supposition that the establishment of the Catholic religion was one of the objects of this rebellion, is proved to be unfounded, by the evidence of the principal leaders, Emmet and M'Nevin.

The following are their answers, given before the committees, to the question, "Whether or "not they would set up the Catholic religion?"

 M'Nevin.

ject to endeavour to compose. His Excellency therefore desires me to request, that, in any future edition of the book, the permission to dedicate it to him may be omitted.

I have, &c. E. Littlehales.

* See Dr. Caulfield's Reply to Sir R. Musgrave, sold by Keating and Co. Duke-street.

M'Nevin—" I would no more consent to that, " than to the establishment of Mahometanism."

Emmet—" I do not think the Catholics would " wish to set up a Catholic establishment, even at " the present day. Perhaps some old priests, " who have long groaned under the penal laws, " might wish for a retribution to themselves, but " I don't think the young priests wish for it; and " I am convinced the laity would not submit to it; " and that the objections to it will be every day " gaining strength."

Two circumstances more only remain to be taken notice of regarding the conduct of the Catholics as a body in this rebellion. One of them, the indisputable fact, that, of the twenty-four leaders of the rebellion who were banished to fort St. George, only four of them were Catholics, twelve were of the Church of England, and the remaining eight were Dissenters. Well indeed, then, might Mr. Pitt say, in the House of Commons in 1805, whose opinion is the other circumstance alluded to, " I do not consider the late

" rebellion

"rebellion in Ireland to have been a Catholic "rebellion."*

Facts, reafon, and authority, therefore, it appears, all coincide in the condemnation of the calumny, which a few blind and miftaken men have had juft talent enough to propagate amongft the ignorant and prejudiced. The magna vis veritatis will, however, prevail on this, as well as upon all other occafions, and fooner or later bring forward the unfortunate and much injured Catholics of Ireland to the view of their Englifh fellow-fubjects, as highly deferving of their confidence and their affection.

The next great event belonging to the Catholic queftion is the meafure of union, not as having, in any way, altered the political condition of the Catholics in refpect to the penal laws, but as a meafure concerning which a compact was virtually entered into between them and the Englifh government. For though it is true that no regular articles, like thofe of Limerick, can be produced to prove this compact, ftill there is circumftantial evidence

* Debates on Catholic petition, by Cuthel and Martin, p. 126.

evidence of ſuch a nature as to bring conviction to every candid mind, that, on the one hand, the Catholics did agree to ſupport the union, and, on the other, that the Engliſh government, on their part, did indirectly agree to ſecure to them, in conſideration of that ſupport, the meaſure of emancipation.

This evidence is to be collected; 1ſt. From the ſpeech of Mr. Pitt on propoſing the union articles to the Houſe of Commons; 2d. From the act of union; 3d. From Mr. Pitt's ſpeech, and the letters of Lord Cornwallis and Lord Caſtlereagh, concerning the change of adminiſtration in 1801.

1ſt. Mr. Pitt's ſpeech—" I am well aware," ſays Mr. Pitt, " that the ſubject of religious diſ-
" tinction is a dangerous and delicate topic, eſpe-
" cially when applied to a country ſuch as Ire-
" land; the ſituation of which, in this reſpect, is
" different from every other. Where the eſta-
" bliſhed religion of the ſtate is the ſame as the
" general religion of the empire, and where the
" property of the country is in the hands of a
" comparatively ſmall number of perſons profeſ-

"ſing that religion, while the religion of a great
"majority of the people is different, it is not eaſy
"to ſay, on general principles, what ſyſtem of
"church eſtabliſhment, in ſuch a country, would
"be free from difficulty and inconvenience. By
"many I know it will be contended, that the re-
"ligion profeſſed by the majority of the people
"would, at leaſt, be entitled to an equality of
"privileges. I have heard ſuch an argument
"urged in this Houſe; but thoſe who apply it
"without qualification to the caſe of Ireland, for-
"get ſurely the principles on which Engliſh inte-
"reſt and Engliſh connection has been eſtabliſhed
"in that country, and its preſent legiſlature is
"formed. No man can ſay, that, in the preſent
"ſtate of things, and *while Ireland remains a*
"*ſeparate kingdom, full conceſſions could be made*
"*to the Catholics without endangering the ſtate,*
"*and ſhaking the conſtitution to its centre.*"

Is not this as much as to ſay, that, after an incorporate union ſhall have taken place, theſe FULL CONCESSIONS *could be made* without endangering Ireland? Could theſe words be underſtood in any other way by the Catholics? and,

Are

Are they not an indirect offer, on the part of Mr. Pitt, to the Catholics to make these FULL CONCESSIONS, provided they would enable him to make them without endangering Ireland? But the language which he next employs is stronger and still more in point. He immediately proceeds, "On the other hand, without anticipating the "discussion, or the propriety of agitating the "question, or saying how soon or how late it may "be fit to discuss it, two propositions are indisput- "able—1st. When the conduct of the Catholics "shall be such as to make it safe for the govern- "ment to admit them to the participation of the "privileges granted to those of the established "religion, and when the temper of the times "shall be favourable to such a measure: when "those events take place, it is obvious that such "a question may be agitated in an United Impe- "rial Parliament, with much greater safety than "it could be in a separate legislature. In the "second place, I think it certain, that even for "whatever period it may be thought necessary, "after the union, to withhold from the Catholics "the enjoyment of those advantages, many of the "objections which at present arise out of their "situation

"situation would be removed, if the Protestant "legislature were no longer separate and local, "but general and impartial."

The speech, from which the foregoing is extracted, was circulated gratis by government throughout all Ireland. It was considered by the Catholics as a tender of emancipation; it was anxiously read by all who could read. At the Castle it was explained, to those who sought for explanation, as an unequivocal offer of every concession; and, in the result, the Catholics opposed their own Parliament, and gave their support to Mr. Pitt; and, by the aid of this support, he was enabled to contend with a majority in the House of Commons, and to carry the measure.

We come now to the evidence to be collected from the Act of Union.

Many of the leading Catholics have not hesitated to declare, that the oath prescribed by this act, to qualify members of Parliament on taking their seats, was framed under an arrangement, that, immediately after the measure was passed, they were to enjoy the privilege of fitting in Parliament. The act runs thus, "That every one "of the Lords and Commons of Parliament of "the United Kingdom, and every member of the "House of Commons of the United Kingdom, in "the first and every succeeding Parliament, shall, "*until the Parliament of the United Kingdom shall* "*otherwise provide*, take the oaths as now en- "joined to be taken." "Do not quibble with "us," the Catholics say, "concerning terms and "formalities; it was clearly understood between "us, that if we co-operated to bring about the "union, as we actually did, you would effect the "emancipation. To give a colouring to this en- "gagement, you inserted in the articles of union "an intimation of a proposed change of the oaths "in our favour: when, behold! now you roundly "tell us, that this alteration never shall take place, "and that we must make up our minds to wear "our shackles till the end of time."*

The third head of evidence is Mr. Pitt's speech on explaining the cause of his resignation in 1801, and the letters of Pitt and Lord Cornwallis.

"As

* Dr. Milner's Inquiry, p. 68.

" As to the merits," Mr. Pitt faid, " of the quef-
" tion which led to my refignation, I am willing
" to fubmit them to the Houfe. I and fome of
" my colleagues in office, did feel it an incumbent
" duty upon us to propofe a meafure on the part
" of government, which, *under the circumftances*
" *of the union* fo happily effected between the
" two countries, we thought of great public im-
" portance, and neceffary *to complete* the benefits
" likely to refult from that meafure; we felt this
" opinion fo ftrongly, that, when we met with
" circumftances which rendered it impoffible for
" us to propofe it as a meafure of government, we
" felt it equally inconfiftent with our duty and
" our honour any longer to remain a part of that
" government. What may be the opinion of
" others, I know not, but I beg to have it under-
" ftood to be a meafure which, if I had remained
" in government, I *muft* have propofed."*

Why *muft* Mr. Pitt have propofed this meafure? To this queftion one anfwer alone can be given, becaufe his honour, as a ftatefman, was fubftantially engaged to the Catholics, that, if they

 fupported

* Debrit's Debates, 14, 161.

ſupported the union, he would propoſe emancipation.

We now come to the written communications which, at this time, were made to the Catholics by Mr. Pitt and Lord Cornwallis, and which were given by Lord Caſtlereagh to Dr. Troy, and which are to the following effect:

"The leading part of his Majeſty's Miniſters finding inſurmountable obſtacles to the bringing forward meaſures of conceſſion to the Catholic body, whilſt in office, have felt it impoſſible to continue in adminiſtration under the inability to propoſe it with the circumſtances neceſſary to carrying the meaſure with all its advantages, and they have retired from his Majeſty's ſervice, conſidering this line of conduct as moſt likely to contribute to its ultimate ſucceſs. The Catholic body will, therefore, ſee how much their future hopes muſt depend upon ſtrengthening their cauſe by good conduct in the mean time; they will prudently conſider their proſpects as ariſing from the perſons who now eſpouſe their intereſts, and compare them with thoſe, which they could look to from any other quarter; they may with confidence rely on the zealous ſupport of all thoſe who retire, and of many who remain in office, when it can be given with a proſpect of ſucceſs. They may be aſſured that Mr. Pitt will do his utmoſt to eſtabliſh their cauſe in the public favour, and prepare the way for their finally attaining their objects: and the Catholics will feel, that as Mr. Pitt could not concur in a hopeleſs attempt to force it now, that he muſt at all times repreſs, with the ſame deciſion as if he held an adverſe opinion, any unconſtitutional conduct in the Catholic body.

"Under

"Under these circumstances, it cannot be doubted that the "Catholics will take the most loyal, dutiful, and patient line "of conduct, that they will not suffer themselves to be led "into measures which can, by any construction, give a handle "to the opposers of their wishes, either to misinterpret their "principles, or to raise an argument for resisting their claims; "but that by their prudent and exemplary demeanour they "will afford additional grounds to the growing number of "their advocates to enforce their claims on proper occasions, "until their objects can be finally and advantageously attained.

" *The Sentiments of a sincere Friend (i. e. Marquis Cornwallis) to* " *the Catholic claims.*

"If the Catholics should now proceed to violence, or en- "tertain any ideas of gaining their object by convulsive mea- "sures, or forming associations with men of jacobinical prin- "ciples, they must of course lose the support and aid of those, "who have sacrificed their own situations in their cause, but "who would at the same time feel it to be their indispensable "duty to oppose every thing tending to confusion.

"On the other hand, should the Catholics be sensible of "the benefit they possess, by having so many characters of "eminence pledged not to embark in the service of govern- "ment, except on the terms of the Catholic privileges being "obtained, it is to be hoped, that, on balancing the advan- "tages and disadvantages of their situation, they would prefer "a quiet and peaceable demeanour to any line of conduct of "an opposite description."

The originals of these two declarations were handed to Dr. Troy and afterwards to Lord Fingal on the same day, by Marquis Cornwallis,

in

in the presence of Lieutenant-Colonel Littlehales, in the beginning of May, 1801, shortly before his departure from the government of Ireland, and before the arrival of Lord Hardwicke, his successor. His Excellency desired they should be discreetly communicated to the Bishops and principal Catholics, but not inserted in the newspapers. They appeared, neverthelefs, in the English prints soon afterwards, and were copied into the Irish papers.

Under circumstances such as these, is it surprising that the Catholics should now feel that faith has been broken with them by the government of England? Mr. Pitt, so long ago as in Lord Westmorland's administration, had made no hesitation to say, in such a manner that his sentiments might be known to the Catholics, that he would not risk a rebellion by withholding emancipation. In 1795, he sent Lord Fitzwilliam to Ireland to carry this measure into effect; and, in 1799, he held forth, in language not to be misunderstood, this measure, as the reward which he would give the Catholics for their support to the union. At this time he had governed England, for 14 years, more

more like a despotic Prince, than a Minister of a King over a free people; he was supported by great majorities in Parliament, and he possessed the unbounded confidence of the King. What other construction, then, could his language on the union bear, among the Catholics, than that of a positive engagement on the part of England to give them emancipation, provided they gave the union, in the first instance, their support? No one can say that they formed their expectations that this measure would be conceded to them without good grounds for doing so; and there being good grounds, no correct moralist can maintain that England made no such engagement.

Having now traced the history of the penal laws and the Catholics, from the treaty of Limerick down to the union, it remains only to make a conclusion of this work, by collecting the several inferences which may be drawn from the facts contained in it.

In the first place, the Catholics have to complain of a distinct breach of faith by the government of England.

Secondly, They have to complain of having endured a greater ſhare of inſult and of oppreſſion than it ever was the lot of any other people in any other country to be expoſed to.

Thirdly, They have it in their power to repel all thoſe charges which have been made againſt them for being diſloyal to the Houſe of Brunſwick, 1ſt. By their conduct in 1715; 2dly, By their conduct in 1745; 3dly, By their conduct during the American war; and, laſtly, By their conduct in 1798.

Fourthly, They have it in their power to ſhew, that their clergy have, at all times, inculcated ſound doctrines of morality, of peace and ſubmiſſion to the government, and of brotherly affection for their Proteſtant fellow countrymen.

Fifthly, They can prove that their religious principles have been wholly miſunderſtood; and that they are not, in any degree, repugnant with their duty as loyal ſubjects.*

Sixthly,

* Vide Appendix, No. 3. and No. 4. and Note B.

And, laſtly, it may be laid down as incontrovertibly proved, that the penal code is the ſole cauſe of any inferiority which can now be diſcovered in the ſtate and condition of Ireland, as compared with the ſtate and condition of any other country, whether in reſpect to the poverty, the ignorance, the miſery, or the diſpoſition of the loweſt orders of her inhabitants, or to any other circumſtance which enables England to boaſt her more advanced progreſs in refinement and civilization. To the penal code it is that England has to look for the ſource of all alarm ſhe now entertains for the ſafety of Ireland; and to England Ireland has to look for the cauſe of all the miſery and degradation which, at this day even, peculiarly mark her character among the nations of the world. Yet it is ſome conſolation to reflect, that Ireland contains in herſelf a healing principle, in the liberality which the Iriſh Proteſtants have lately diſplayed in ſupport of the claims of their Catholic countrymen. A ſupport which has nobly vindicated the origin which the Proteſtant Church deduces from reaſon and toleration.*

* Vide Note 6.

It ſhews that the bigotry, which there have been ſo much miſchievous pains taken to excite, is not natural to Iriſhmen. Indeed, what vice is leſs congenial to the Iriſh character than bigotry? Bigotry is gloomy and excluſive, the Iriſh character is chearful and ſocial; bigotry is perverſe and diſingenuous, querulous, ſour, and malignant; the Iriſh character is candid, full of quick, expanding ſympathy, kind and facile to a fault, ſlow to hatred, free from ſuſpicion and captiouſneſs. The tint of bigotry that it has worn is not its complexion, but the ſtains that have tarniſhed its native hue; even theſe are not fixed nor permanent—they bleach and fade in the light, and, to be entirely effaced, require nothing but conſtant expoſure.

APPENDIX.

No. I.

The ſeveral Arguments of Sir Theobald Butler, Counſellor Malone, and Sir Stephen Rice, at the Bar of the Houſe of Commons of Ireland, February 22d; and at the Bar of the Houſe of Lords, February 28th, 1703, againſt paſſing the Bill entitled, An Act to prevent the further Growth of Popery.

THE papiſts of Ireland obſerving that the Houſe of Commons were preparing the heads of a bill, to be tranſmitted to England, to be drawn up into an act, *to prevent the further growth of popery*, and having in vain endeavoured to put a ſtop to it there; at its remittance back again to Ireland, preſented to the Houſe of Commons a petition, in the names of Nicholas Lord Viſcount Kingſland, Colonel J. Brown, Colonel Burk, Colonel Robert Nugent, Major Pat. Allen, Captain Arthur French, and other Roman Catholics of Ireland, praying to be heard by their counſel againſt the paſſing the ſaid bill, then under conſideration of the ſaid Houſe; and to have a copy of the bill, and a reaſonable time to ſpeak to it before it paſſed. Which petition being referred to the committee of the whole Houſe, to whom the conſideration of the ſaid bill was referred, it was ordered, that the petitioners ſhould have a copy of the ſaid bill, and be heard by their counſel, before the ſaid committee.

And, in purſuance of that order, Sir Theobald Butler, Counſellor Malone, and Sir Stephen Rice, (the two firſt in their gowns as counſel for the petitioners in general, and the laſt without a gown, only as a petitioner in his private capacity), together with many others, upon Tueſday the 22d of February, 1703, appeared at the bar of the ſaid Houſe of Commons, where Sir Theobald Butler firſt moved and acquainted the Houſe, that, " by the permiſſion of that Houſe, he was come thither in behalf of himſelf, and the reſt of the Roman Catholics of Ireland comprifed in the *Articles of Limerick* and *Galway*, to offer fome reafons, which he and the reft of the petitioners judged very material againft paffing the bill, entitled, *An act to prevent the further growth of popery;* that, by leave of the Houfe, he had taken a copy of the faid bill (which he had there in his hand), and, with fubmiffion, looked upon it to tend to the deftroying of the faid articles, granted upon the moft valuable confiderations of furrendering the faid garrifons, at a time when they had the fword in their hands; and, for any thing that appeared to the contrary, might have been in a condition to hold out much longer, and when it was in their power to demand, and make for themfelves fuch terms, as might be for their then future liberty, fafety, and fecurity; and that, too, when the allowing fuch terms were highly advantageous to the government to which they fubmitted; as well for uniting the people that were then divided, quieting and fettling the diftractions and diforders of this then miferable kingdom, as for the other advantages the government would thereby reap in its own affairs, both at home and abroad; when its enemies were fo powerful both by fea and land, as to give doubt of interruption to its peace and fettlement.

" That, by fuch their power, thofe of Limerick did for themfelves, and others comprifed, obtain, and make fuch articles, as by which, all the Irifh inhabitants in the city and county of Limerick, and in the counties of Clare, Kerry, Cork, Sligo, and Mayo, had full and free pardon of and for all attainders, outlawries, treafons, mifprifion of treafons, felonies, trefpaffes, and other crimes whatever, which at any time from the beginning of King James the Second, to the 3d of October, 1691, had been acted, committed, or done by them, or any of them; and by which they and their heirs were to be forthwith put in poffeffion of, and for ever poffefs, and enjoy all and every of their freeholds and inheritance; and all their rights, titles, and interefts, privileges and immunities, which they and every of them held and enjoyed, and by the laws in force were entitled unto, in the reign of King Charles II. or at any time fince, by the laws and ftatutes that were in force in that reign, &c. And thereupon read fo much of the fecond article of Limerick, as tended to that purpofe.

" That in the reign of King Charles the Second, the petitioners, and all that were entitled to the benefit of thofe articles, were in fuch full and free poffeffion of their eftates; and had the fame power to fell, or otherwife to difpofe, or convey them, or any other thing they enjoyed; and were as rightfully entitled to all the privileges, immunities, and other advantages whatever, according

according to the laws then in force, as any other ſubjects whatſoever, and which, therefore, without the higheſt injuſtice, could not be taken from them, unleſs they had forfeited them themſelves.

"That if they had made any ſuch forfeiture, it was either before or after the making of the ſaid articles: if before, they had a full and free pardon for that by the ſaid articles, &c. and therefore are not accountable by any law now in force for the ſame, and for that reaſon not now to be charged with it; and ſince they cannot be charged with any general forfeiture of thoſe articles ſince, they at the ſame time remained as abſolutely entitled to all the privileges, advantages, and benefits of the laws both already made, and hereafter to be made, as any other of her Majeſty's ſubjects whatſoever.

"That among all ſocieties there were ſome ill people, but that, by the 10th article of Limerick, the whole community is not to be charged with, nor forfeit by, the crimes of particular perſons.

"That there were already wholeſome laws in force ſufficient, and if not, ſuch as were wanting might be made, to puniſh every offender according to the nature of the crime: and in the name of God let the guilty ſuffer for their own faults; but the innocent ought not to ſuffer for the guilty, nor the whole for any particular. That ſurely they would not now (they had tamely got the ſword out of their hands) rob them of what was in their power to have kept; for that would be unjuſt, and not according to that golden rule, to do as they would be done by, was the caſe reverſed, and the contrary ſide their own.

"That the ſaid articles were firſt granted them by the general of the Engliſh army, upon the moſt important conſideration of getting the city of Limerick into his hands (when it was in a condition to have held out, till it might have been relieved by the ſuccours then coming to it from France) and for preventing the further effuſion of blood, and the other ill conſequences which (by reaſon of the then diviſions and diſorders) the nation then laboured under; and for reducing thoſe in arms againſt the Engliſh government to its obedience.

"That the ſaid articles were ſigned and perfected by the ſaid general, and the then lords juſtices of this kingdom: and afterwards ratified by their late Majeſties, for themſelves, their heirs and ſucceſſors: and have been ſince confirmed by an act of Parliament in this kingdom, viz. ſtat. 9. Guil. 3. ſes. 4. chap. 27. (which he there produced and pleaded), and ſaid could not be avoided without breaking the ſaid articles, and the public faith thereby plighted to all thoſe compriſed under the ſaid articles,

in

in the moſt ſolemn and engaging manner it is poſſible for any people to lay themſelves under; and than which nothing could be more ſacred and binding. That therefore to violate, or break thoſe articles, would on the contrary be the greateſt injuſtice poſſible for any one people of the whole world to inflict upon another, and which is contrary to both the laws of God and man.

" That, purſuant to theſe articles, all thoſe Iriſh then in arms againſt the government did ſubmit thereunto, and ſurrendered the ſaid city of Limerick, and all other garriſons then remaining in their poſſeſſion; and did take ſuch oaths of fidelity to the King and Queen, &c. as by the ſaid articles they were obliged to, and were put into poſſeſſion of their eſtates, &c.

" That ſuch their ſubmiſſion was upon ſuch terms, as ought now, and at all times, to be made good to them: but that if the bill then before the Houſe, entitled, An act to prevent the further growth of popery, ſhould paſs into a law (which, ſaid he, God forbid!) it would be not only a violation of thoſe articles, but alſo a manifeſt breach of the public faith, of which the Engliſh had always been moſt tender in many inſtances, ſome of which he there quoted; and that, in particular, in the preamble of the act before mentioned, made for confirmation of theſe articles, wherein there is a particular regard and reſpect had to the public faith.

" That ſince the ſaid articles were thus under the moſt ſolemn ties, and for ſuch valuable conſiderations granted the petitioners, by nothing leſs than the General of the army, the Lords Juſtices of the kingdom, the King, Queen, and Parliament, the public faith of the nation was therein concerned, obliged, bound, and engaged, as fully and firmly as was poſſible for one people to pledge faith to another; that therefore this Parliament could not paſs ſuch a bill, as that entitled, An act to prevent the further growth of popery, then before the Houſe, into a law, without infringing thoſe articles, and a manifeſt breach of the public faith; of which he hoped that Houſe would be no leſs regardful and tender than their predeceſſors, who made the act for confirming thoſe articles, had been.

" That the caſe of the Gibeonites, 2 Sam. xxi. 1. was a fearful example of breaking of public faith, which, above 100 years after, brought nothing leſs than a three years famine upon the land, and ſtayed not till the lives of all Saul's family atoned for it.

" That even among the heathens, and moſt barbarous of nations all the world over, the public faith had always been held moſt ſacred and binding, that ſurely it would find no leſs a regard in that auguſt aſſembly.

" That

" That if he proved that the passing that act was such a manifest breach of those articles, and consequently of the public faith, he hoped that honourable House would be very tender how they passed the said bill before them into a law, to the apparent prejudice of the petitioners, and the hazard of bringing upon themselves and posterity such evils, reproach, and infamy, as the doing the like had brought upon other nations and people.

" Now, that the passing such a bill as that then before the House, to prevent *the further growth of popery*, will be a breach of those articles, and consequently of the public faith, I prove (said he) by the following argument.

" The argument then is (said he) whatever shall be enacted to the prejudice or destroying of any obligation, covenant, or contract, in the most solemn manner, and for the most valuable consideration entered into, is a manifest violation and destruction of every such obligation, covenant, and contract; but the passing that bill into a law will evidently and absolutely destroy the articles of Limerick and Galway, to all intents and purposes, and therefore the passing that bill into a law will be such a breach of those articles, and consequently of the public faith plighted for performing those articles, which remained to be proved.

" The major is proved (said he), for that whatever destroys or violates any contract or obligation, upon the most valuable considerations, most solemnly made and entered into, destroys and violates the end of every such contract or obligation; but the end and design of those articles was, that all those therein comprised, and every of their heirs, should hold, possess, and enjoy all and every of their estates of freehold and inheritance, and all the rights, titles, and interests, privileges and immunities, which they and every of them held, enjoyed, or were rightfully entitled to, in the reign of King Charles the Second; or at any time since, by the laws and statutes that were in force in the said reign in this realm: but that the design of this bill was to take away every such right, title, interest, &c. from every father being a papist, and to make the popish father, who, by the articles and laws aforesaid, had an undoubted right, either to sell or otherwise at pleasure to dispose of his estate, at any time of his life, as he thought fit; only tenant for life; and consequently disabled from selling, or otherwise disposing thereof, after his son or other heir should become protestant; though otherwise never so disobedient, profligate, or extravagant: Ergo, this act tends to the destroying the end for which those articles were made, and consequently the breaking of the public faith, plighted for their performance.

" The

"The minor is proved by the 3d, 4th, 5th, 6th, 7th, 8th, 9th, 15th, 16th, and 17th clauſes of the ſaid bill, all which (ſaid he) I ſhall conſider and ſpeak to, in the order as they are placed in the bill.

"By the firſt of theſe clauſes (which is the third of the bill), I that am the popiſh father, without committing any crime againſt the ſtate, or the laws of the land, (by which only I ought to be governed) or any other fault; but merely for being of the religion of my forefathers, and that which, till of late years, was the ancient religion of theſe kingdoms, contrary to the expreſs words of the ſecond article of Limerick, and the public faith plighted as aforeſaid for their performance; am deprived of my inheritance, freehold, &c. and of all other advantages, which, by thoſe articles, and the laws of the land, I am entitled to enjoy, equally with every other of my fellow-ſubjects, whether proteſtant or popiſh. And though ſuch my eſtate be even the purchaſe of my own hard labour and induſtry, yet I ſhall not (though my occaſions be never ſo preſſing) have liberty (after my eldeſt ſon or other heir becomes a proteſtant) to ſell, mortgage, or otherwiſe diſpoſe of, or charge it for payment of my debts; or have leave, out of my own eſtate, to order portions for my other children; or leave a legacy, though never ſo ſmall, to my poor father or mother, or other poor relations; but during my own life, my eſtate ſhall be given to my ſon or other heir, being a proteſtant, though never ſo undutiful, profligate, extravagant, or otherwiſe undeſerving; and I that am the purchaſing father ſhall become tenant, for life only, to my own purchaſe, inheritance, and freehold, which I purchaſed with my own money; and ſuch my ſon or other heir, by this act, ſhall be at liberty to ſell, or otherwiſe at pleaſure to diſpoſe of my eſtate, the ſweat of my brows, before my face; and I that am the purchaſer, ſhall not have liberty to raiſe one farthing upon the eſtate of my own purchaſe, either to pay my debts or portion my daughters (if any I have), or make proviſions for my other male children, though never ſo deſerving and dutiful: but my eſtate, and the iſſues and profits of it, ſhall, before my face, be at the diſpoſal of another, who cannot poſſibly know how to diſtinguiſh between the dutiful and undutiful, deſerving or undeſerving. Is not this, gentlemen, (ſaid he), a hard caſe? I beſeech you, gentlemen, to conſider, whether you would not think ſo, if the ſcale was changed, and the caſe your own, as it is like to be ours, if this bill paſs into a law.

"It is natural for the father to love the child, but we all know (ſays he) that children are but too apt and ſubject, without any ſuch liberty as this bill gives, to ſlight and neglect their duty to their parents; and surely such an act as this will not be an instrument of restraint, but rather encourage them more to it.

"It is but too common with the son, who has a prospect of an estate, when once he arrives at the age of one and twenty, to think the old father too long in the way between him and it; and how much more will he be subject to it, when, by this act, he shall have liberty, before he comes to that age, to compel and force my estate from me, without asking my leave, or being liable to account with me for it, or out of his share thereof, to a moiety of the debts, portions, or other incumbrances, with which the estate might have been charged before the passing this act.

"Is not this against the laws of God and man? against the rules of reason and justice; by which all men ought to be governed? Is not this the only way in the world to make children become undutiful? and to bring the grey head of the parent to the grave with grief and tears?

"It would be hard from any man; but from a son, a child, the fruit of my body, whom I have nurst in my bosom, and tendered more dearly than my own life, to become my plunderer, to rob me of my estate, to cut my throat, and to take away my bread, is much more grievous than from any other; and enough to make the most flinty of hearts to bleed to think on it. And yet this will be the case if this bill pass into a law; which I hope this honourable assembly will not think of, when they shall more seriously consider, and have weighed these matters.

"For God's sake, gentlemen, will you consider whether this is according to the golden rule, to do as you would be done unto? And if not, surely you will not, nay you cannot, without being liable to be charged with the most manifest injustice imaginable, take from us our birth-rights, and invest them in others before our faces.

"By the 4th clause of the bill, the popish father is under the penalty of 500l. debarred from being guardian to, or having the tuition or custody of his own child or children; but if the child pretends to be a protestant, though never so young, or incapable of judging of the principles of any religion, it shall be taken from its own father, and put into the hands or care of a protestant relation, if any there be qualified as this act directs, for tuition, though never so great an enemy to the popish parent; and for want of relations so qualified, into the hands and tuition of such protestant stranger as the court of chancery shall think fit to appoint; who perhaps may likewise be my enemy, and out of prejudice to me, who am the popiſh father, ſhall infuſe into my child, not only ſuch principles of religion as are wholly inconſiſtent with my liking, but alſo againſt the duty which, by the laws both of God and nature, is due from every child to its parents: And it ſhall not be in my power to remedy, or queſtion him for it; and yet I ſhall be obliged to pay for ſuch education, how pernicious ſoever. Nay, if a legacy or eſtate fall to any of my children, being minors, I that am the popiſh father ſhall not have the liberty to take care of it, but it ſhall be put into the hands of a ſtranger; and though I ſee it confounded before my face, it ſhall not be in my power to help it. Is not this a hard caſe, gentlemen? I am ſure you cannot but allow it to be a very hard caſe.

"The 5th clauſe provides, that no proteſtant or proteſtants, having any eſtate real or perſonal, within this kingdom, ſhall, at any time after the 24th of March, 1703, intermarry with any papiſt, either in or out of this kingdom, under the penalties in an act made in the 9th of King William, entitled, An act to prevent proteſtants intermarrying with papiſts; which penalties ſee in the 5th clauſe of the act itſelf.

"Surely, gentlemen, this is ſuch a law as was never heard of before, and againſt the law of right, and the law of nations; and therefore a law which is not in the power of mankind to make, without breaking through the laws which our wiſe anceſtors prudently provided for the ſecurity of poſterity, and which you cannot infringe without hazarding the undermining the whole legiſlature, and encroaching upon the privileges of your neighbouring nations, which it is not reaſonable to believe they will allow.

"It has indeed been known, that there hath been laws made in England that have been binding in Ireland; but ſurely it never was known, that any law made in Ireland could affect England or any other country. But, by this act, a perſon committing matrimony (an ordinance of the Almighty) in England, or any other part beyond the ſeas (where it is lawful both by the laws of God and man ſo to do) if ever they come to live in Ireland, and have an inheritance or title to any intereſt to the value of 500l. they ſhall be puniſhed for a fact conſonant with the laws of the land where it was committed. But, gentlemen, by your favour, this is what, with ſubmiſſion, is not in your power to do; for no law that either now is, or that hereafter ſhall be in force in this kingdom, ſhall be able to take cognizance of any fact committed in another nation: nor can any one nation make laws for any other nation, but what is ſubordinate to it, as Ireland is to England; but no other nation is ſubordinate

ordinate to Ireland, and therefore any laws made in Ireland cannot punish me for any fact committed in any other nation, but more especially England, to whom Ireland is subordinate. And the reason is, every free nation, such as all our neighbouring nations are, by the great law of nature, and the universal privileges of all nations, have an undoubted right to make, and be ruled and governed by laws of their own making; for that, to submit to any other, would be to give away their own birth-right and native freedom, and become subordinate to their neighbours, as we of this kingdom, since the making of Poyning's act, have been, and are to England. A right which England would never so much as endure to hear of, much less to submit to.

"We see how careful our forefathers have been to provide that no man shall be punished in one county (even of the same nation) for crimes committed in another county; and surely it would be highly unreasonable, and contrary to the laws of all nations in the whole world, to punish me in this kingdom for a fact committed in England, or any other nation, which was not against, but consistent with the laws of the nation where it was committed. I am sure there is not any law in any other nation of the world that would do it.

"The 6th clause of this bill is likewise a manifest breach of the second of Limerick articles; for, by that article, all persons comprised under those articles were to enjoy, and have the full benefit of, all the rights, titles, privileges, and immunities whatsoever, which they enjoyed, or by the laws of the land then in force were entitled to enjoy, in the reign of King Charles II. And by the laws then in force, all the papists of Ireland had the same liberty that any of their fellow-subjects had, to purchase any manors, lands, tenements, hereditaments, leases of lives, or for years, rents, or any other thing of profit whatsoever; but by this clause of this bill, every papist or person professing the popish religion, after the 24th of March, 1703, is made incapable of purchasing any manors, lands, tenements, hereditaments, or any rents or profits out of the same; or holding any lease of lives, or any other lease whatsoever, for any term exceeding thirty-one years; wherein a rent, not less than two-thirds of the improved yearly value, shall be reserved, and made payable during the whole term; and, therefore, this clause of this bill, if made into a law, will be a manifest breach of those articles.

"The 7th clause is yet of much more general consequence, and not only a like breach of those articles, but also a manifest robbing of all the Roman catholics of the kingdom of their birth-right; for, by those articles, all those therein comprised were (said he) pardoned all misdemeanours whatsoever, of which they had in any manner of way been guilty; and restored to all the rights, liberties, privileges, and immunities whatever, which, by the laws of the land, and customs, constitutions, and native birth-right, they, any, and every of them, were, equally with every other of their fellow-subjects, entitled unto. And by the laws of nature and nations, as well as by the laws of the land, every native of any country has an undoubted right and just title to all the privileges and advantages which such their native country affords: And surely no man but will allow, that, by such a native right, every one born in any country hath an undoubted right to the inheritance of his father, or any other, to whom he or they may be heir at law; but if this bill pass into a law, every native of this kingdom, that is, and shall remain a papist, is, *ipso facto*, during life, or his or their continuing a papist, deprived of such inheritance, devise, gift, remainder, or trust, of any lands, tenements, or hereditaments, of which any protestant now is, or hereafter shall be seized in fee-simple absolute, or fee-tail, which, by the death of such protestant, or his wife, ought to descend immediately to his son or sons, or other issue in tail, being such papists, and 18 years of age; or, if under that age, within six months after coming to that age, shall not conform to the church of Ireland, as by law established; and every such devise, gift, remainder, or trust, which, according to the laws of the land, and such native right, ought to descend to such papist, shall, during the life of such papist (unless he forsake his religion) descend to the nearest relation that is a protestant, and his heirs, being and continuing protestants, as though the said popish heir and all other popish relations were dead; without being accountable for the same: which is nothing less than robbing such popish heir of such his birth-right: for no other reason, but his being and continuing of that religion, which by the first of Limerick articles, the Roman catholics of this kingdom were to enjoy, as they did in the reign of King Charles II. and then there was no law in force, that deprived any Roman catholic of this kingdom of any such their native birth-right, or any other thing, which, by the laws of the land then in force, any other fellow-subjects were entitled unto.

"The 8th clause of this bill, is to erect in this kingdom a law of *gavel-kind*, a law in itself so monstrous and strange, that I dare say, this is the first time it was ever heard of in the world; a law so pernicious and destructive to the well-being of families and societies, that, in an age or two, there will hardly be any remembrance of any of the ancient Roman catholic families

known

known in the kingdom: a law which, therefore, I may again venture to ſay, was never before known or heard of in the univerſe!

"There is, indeed, in Kent, a cuſtom, called the Cuſtom of Gavelkind; but I never heard of any law for it till now; and that cuſtom is far different from what by this bill is intended to be made a law; for there, and by that cuſtom, the father, or other perſon, dying poſſeſſed of any eſtate of his own acquiſition, or not entailed, (let him be of what perſuaſion he will), may by will bequeath it at pleaſure: Or if he dies without will, the eſtate ſhall not be divided, if there be any male heir to inherit it; but for want of male heir, then it ſhall deſcend in Gavelkind among the daughters, and not otherwiſe. But by this act, for want of a proteſtant heir, enrolled as ſuch within three months after the death of ſuch papiſt, to be divided, ſhare and ſhare alike, among all his ſons; for want of ſons, among his daughters; for want of ſuch, among the collateral kindred of his father; and in want of ſuch, among thoſe of his mother; and this is to take place of any grant, ſettlement, &c. other than ſale, for valuable conſideration of money, really, *bona fide*, paid. And ſhall I not call this a ſtrange law? Surely it is a ſtrange law, which, contrary to the laws of all nations, thus confounds all ſettlements, how ancient ſoever, or otherwiſe warrantable by all the laws heretofore in force, in this, or any other kingdom!

"The 9th clauſe of this act, is another manifeſt breach of the articles of Limerick; for, by the 9th of thoſe articles, no oath is to be adminiſtered to, nor impoſed upon ſuch Roman Catholics, as ſhould ſubmit to the government, but the oath of allegiance, appointed by an act of Parliament made in England, in the firſt year of the reign of their late Majeſties King William and Queen Mary, (which is the ſame with the firſt of thoſe appointed by the 10th clauſe of this act:) But by this clauſe, none ſhall have the benefit of this act, that ſhall not conform to the church of Ireland, ſubſcribe the declaration, and take and ſubſcribe the oath of abjuration, appointed by the 9th clauſe of this act; and therefore this act is a manifeſt breach of thoſe articles, &c. and a force upon all the Roman catholics therein compriſed, either to abjure their religion, or part with their birth-rights; which, by thoſe articles, they were, and are, as fully, and as rightfully entitled unto, as any other ſubjects whatever.

"The 10th, 11th, 12th, 13th, and 14th clauſes of this bill, (ſaid he) relate to offices and employments, which the papiſts of Ireland cannot hope for the enjoyment of, otherwiſe than by grace

grace and favour extraordinary; and therefore, do not so much affect them, as it does the protestant dissenters, who (if this bill pass into a law) are equally with the papists deprived of bearing any office, civil or military, under the government, to which by right of birth, and the laws of the land, they are as indisputably entitled, as any other their protestant brethren: And if what the Irish did in the late disorders of this kingdom made them rebels, (which the presence of a King, they had before been obliged to own, and swear obedience to, gave them a reasonable colour of concluding it did not), yet surely the dissenters did not do any thing to make them so; or to deserve worse at the hands of the government, than other protestants; but, on the contrary, it is more than probable, that if they, (I mean the dissenters), had not put a stop to the career of the Irish army at Enniskillen and Londonderry, the settlement of the government, both in England and Scotland, might not have proved so easy, as it thereby did; for if that army had got to Scotland, (as there was nothing at that time to have hindered them, but the bravery of those people, who were mostly dissenters, and chargeable with no other crime since; unless their close adhering to, and early appearing for the then government, and the many faithful services they did their country, were crimes) I say (said he) if they had got to Scotland, when they had boats, barks, and all things else ready for their transportation, and a great many friends there in arms, waiting only their coming to join them; it is easy to think, what the consequence would have been to both these kingdoms; and these dissenters then were thought fit for command, both civil and military, and were no less instrumental in contributing to the reducing the kingdom, than any other protestants: And to pass a bill now, to deprive them of their birth-rights, (for those their good services), would surely be a most unkind return, and the worst reward ever granted to a people so deserving. Whatever the papists may be supposed to have deserved, the dissenters certainly stand as clean in the face of the present government, as any other people whatsoever: And if this is all the return they are like to get, it will be but a slender encouragement, if ever occasion should require, for others to pursue their examples.

"By the 15th, 16th, and 17th clauses of this bill, all papists, after the 24th of March 1703, are prohibited from purchasing any houses or tenements, or coming to dwell in any in Limerick or Galway, or the suburbs of either, and even such as were under the articles, and by virtue thereof have ever since lived there, from staying there; without giving such security as neither those articles, nor any law heretofore in force, do require; except

except ſeamen, fiſhermen, and day-labourers, who pay not above forty ſhillings a year rent; and from voting for the election of members of Parliament, unleſs they take the oath of abjuration; which, to oblige them to, is contrary to the 9th of Limerick articles; which, as aforeſaid, ſays the oath of allegiance, and no other, ſhall be impoſed upon them; and, unleſs they abjure their religion, takes away their advowſons and right of preſentation, contrary to the privilege of right, the law of nations, and the great charter of Magna Charta; which provides, that no man ſhall be diſſeized of his birth-right, without committing ſome crime againſt the known laws of the land in which he is born, or inhabits. And if there was no law in force, in the reign of King Charles the Second, againſt theſe things (as there certainly was not), and if the Roman catholics of this kingdom have not ſince forfeited their right to the laws that then were in force, (as for certain they have not), then with humble ſubmiſſion, all the aforeſaid clauſes and matters contained in this bill, entitled, *An act to prevent the further growth of popery*, are directly againſt the plain words and true intent and meaning of the ſaid articles, and a violation of the public faith, and the laws made for their performance; and what I therefore hope (ſaid he) this honourable houſe will conſider accordingly."

Counſellor Malone and Sir Stephen Rice made diſcourſes on the ſame ſide; the latter, not as a counſel, but as a petitioner, likely to be aggrieved by the paſſing of the ſaid act: But in the courſe of the reply to the arguments of thoſe gentlemen, it was objected, that they had not demonſtrated how and when (ſince the making of the articles of Limerick) the papiſts of Ireland had addreſſed the Queen or government, when all other ſubjects were ſo doing, or had otherwiſe declared their fidelity and obedience to the Queen.

It was (among other things) obſerved, that by a proviſo at the latter end of the ſecond of thoſe articles, none was to have or enjoy the benefit thereof, that ſhould refuſe to take the oath of allegiance.

That any right which the papiſts pretended to be taken from them by the bill, was in their own power to remedy, by conforming; as in prudence, they ought to do; and that they ought not to blame any but themſelves.

The next day the bill was ordered to be engroſſed and ſent to the Lords.

The petitioners having applied to the Lords alſo, for leave to be heard by their counſel againſt the bill, the ſame was granted; and the ſame counſel, upon Monday, February 28th, appeared there, and offered ſuch like arguments as they had made

made uſe of in the other Houſe: They told their Lordſhips, that it had been objected by the Commons, that the paſſing that bill would not be a breach of the articles of Limerick, as had been ſuggeſted: becauſe, the perſons therein compriſed were only to be put into the ſame ſtate they were in the reign of Charles the Second, and becauſe, that in that reign there was no law in force which hindered the paſſing any other law thought needful for the future ſafety of the government. That the Commons had further ſaid, that the paſſing this bill was needful at preſent, for the ſecurity of the kingdom; and that there was not any thing in the articles of Limerick that prohibited their ſo doing.

It was admitted, on the part of the petitioners, that the legiſlative power cannot be confined from altering and making ſuch laws as ſhall be thought neceſſary for ſecuring the quiet and ſafety of the government; that in time of war or danger, or when there ſhall be juſt reaſon to ſuſpect any ill deſigns to diſturb the public peace, no articles or previous obligations ſhall tie up the hands of the legiſlators from providing for its ſafety, or bind the government from diſarming and ſecuring any who may be reaſonably ſuſpected of favouring or correſponding with its enemies, or to be otherwiſe guilty of ill practices: "Or indeed to enact any other law," ſaid Sir Stephen Rice, "that may be abſolutely needful for the ſafety and advantage of the public; ſuch a law cannot be a breach either of theſe, or any other like articles. But then ſuch laws ought to be in general, and ſhould not ſingle out, or affect, any one particular part or party of the people, who gave no provocation to any ſuch law, and whoſe conduct ſtood hitherto unimpeached, ever ſince the ratification of the aforeſaid articles of Limerick.—To make any law that ſhall ſingle any particular part of the people out from the reſt, and take from them what, by right of birth, and all the preceding laws of the land had been confirmed to, and entailed upon them, will be an apparent violation of the original inſtitution of all right, and an ill precedent to any that hereafter might diſlike either the preſent or any other ſettlement, which ſhould be in their power to alter; the conſequence of which is hard to imagine."

The Lord Chancellor having ſummed up all that had been offered at the bar, the Houſe proceeded thereupon; the bill was read through; and, to the great mortification of that unhappy party, was paſſed; and upon the 4th of March obtained the royal aſſent.

No. II.

Declaration of the Catholic Nobility, Gentlemen, and Clergy, May 6, 1798.

Dublin, May 6, 1798.

" To such of the deluded people, now in rebellion against his " Majesty's Government, in this Kingdom, as profess the " Roman Catholic religion.

" THE undersigned Roman Catholics of Ireland feel them- " selves earnestly called on to remonstrate with such of the " deluded people of that persuasion as are now engaged in open " rebellion against his majesty's government, on the wicked " tendency and consequences of the conduct which they have " embraced; they apprehend, with equal horror and concern, " that such deluded men, in addition to the crime committed " against the allegiance which they owe to his majesty, have, " in some instances, attempted to give their designs a colour of " zeal for the religion which they profess. The undersigned " profess equally with them the Roman catholic religion; some " of them are bishops of that persuasion, others are heads of " the leading families who profess that religion; and others are " men of the same persuasion, who, by an honourable industry, " have, under the constitution, now sought to be subverted, " raised themselves to a situation which affords them, in the " most extensive sense, all the comforts of life. The under- " signed of each description concur in entreating such of the " deluded who have taken up arms against the established " government, or entered into engagements tending to that " effect, to return to their allegiance; and, by relinquishing " the treasonable plans in which they are engaged, to entitle " themselves to that mercy which their lawful governors " anxiously wish to extend to them; a contrary conduct will " inevitably subject them to loss of life and property, and ex- " pose their families to ignominy and beggary; whilst at the " same time it will throw on their religion, of which they pro- " fess to be the advocates, the most indelible stain: on this " point, the unfortunately deluded will do well to consider " whether the true interests and honour of the Roman catholic " religion are likely to be most considered by the bishops of

" that persuasion; by the ancient families who profess that reli-
" gion, and who have resisted every temptation to relinquish it;
" by men, who at once professing it, and submitting to the
" present constitution, have arrived at a state of affluence which
" gratifies every wish; or by a set of desperate and profligate
" men, availing themselves of the want of education and expe-
" rience in those whom they seek to use as instruments for grati-
" fying their own wicked and interested views. At all events,
" the undersigned feel themselves bound to rescue their names,
" and, as far as in them lies, the religion which they profess,
" from the ignominy which each would incur, from an appear-
" ance of acquiescence in such criminal and irreligious conduct:
" and they hesitate not to declare, that the accomplishment of
" the views of the deluded of their persuasion, if effected, must
" be effected by the downfall of the clergy, of the ancient fami-
" lies and respectable commercial men of the Roman catholic
" religion, the undersigned individuals of each of which de-
" scription hereby publicly declare their determination to stand
" or fall with the present existing constitution.

" FINGALL,
" GORMANSTOWN,
" SOUTHWELL,
" KENMARE,
" Sir EDWARD BELLEW, with 41 gen-
" tlemen and professors of divinity,
" together with the Rev. PETER
" FLOOD, D. D. president of the
" Royal College of St. Patrick,
" Maynooth, for himself, the pro-
" fessors, and students of said col-
" lege."

No. III.

The principles of the Roman Catholics, from the Prayer Book which is in general uſe amongſt the Catholics of Ireland, and which was publiſhed by Dr. Coppinger, Titular Biſhop of Cloyne.

SECTION I.

1. THE fruition of God, and the remiſſion of ſin, are not attainable by man, otherwiſe than in and by the merits of Jeſus Chriſt, who gratuitouſly purchaſed them for us.

2. Theſe merits of Chriſt are not applied to us otherwiſe than by a right faith in him.

3. This faith is but one, entire and conformable to its object, which is divine revelation, and to which faith gives an undoubting aſſent.

4. This revelation contains many myſteries tranſcending the natural reach of human underſtanding. Wherefore,

5. It became the Divine Wiſdom and Goodneſs to provide ſome way or means whereby man might arrive to the knowledge of theſe myſteries; means viſible and apparent to all; means proportioned to the capacities of all; means ſure and certain to all.

6. *This way or means is not the reading of the Scripture interpreted according to the private reaſon or judgment of each particular perſon or nation;* but,

7. *It is an attention and ſubmiſſion to the voice of the Catholic or univerſal Church eſtabliſhed by Chriſt* for the inſtruction of all; ſpread for that end through all nations, and viſibly continued in the ſucceſſion of paſtors and people through all ages. From this Church, guided in truth, and ſecured from error in matters of faith, by the promiſed aſſiſtance of the Holy Ghoſt, every one may learn the right ſenſe of the Scriptures, and ſuch Chriſtian myſteries and duties as are neceſſary to ſalvation.

8. This church, thus eſtabliſhed, thus ſpread, thus continued, thus guided in one uniform faith, and ſubordination of government, is that which is termed *the Roman Catholic Church;* the qualities juſt mentioned, unity, indeficiency, viſibility, ſucceſſion, and univerſality, being evidently applicable to her.

 9. From

9. From the testimony and authority of this Church, it is that we receive the Scriptures, and believe them to be the word of God: and as she can assuredly tell us what particular book is the word of God, so can she, with the like assurance, tell us also the true sense and meaning of it in controverted points of faith; the same spirit that wrote the Scriptures directs her to understand both them and all matters necessary to salvation. From these grounds it follows:

10. *Only truths revealed by Almighty God, and proposed by the Church, to be believed as such, are, and ought to be, esteemed articles of Catholic faith.*

11. As an obstinate separation from the unity of the Church, in known matters of faith, is heresy; so a wilful separation from the visible unity of the same Church, in matters of subordination and government, is schism.

12. The Church proposes unto us matters of faith, first and chiefly by the Holy Scripture, in points plain and intelligible in it;—secondly, by definitions of general councils, in points not sufficiently plain in Scripture;—thirdly, by apostolical traditions derived from Christ and his Apostles to all succeeding ages.

SECTION II.

1. *The pastors of the Church, who are the body representative, either dispersed or convened in council, have received no commission from Christ to frame new articles of faith, these being solely divine revelation;* but only to explain and to ascertain to us what anciently was and is received and retained as of faith in the Church, when debates and controversies arise about them. These definitions in matters of faith only, and proposed as such, oblige all the Faithful to an interior assent. But,

2. *It is no article of faith that the Church cannot err either in matters of fact, or in matters of speculation or civil policy, depending on mere human reason: these not being divine revelations deposited in the Catholic Church.*—Hence is reduced,

3. If a General Council, much less a Papal Consistory, should presume to depose a King, and to absolve his subjects from their allegiance, no Catholic could be bound to submit to such a decree.—Hence it follows, that,

4. The subjects of the king of England lawfully may, without the least breach of any Catholic principle, renounce, upon oath, the teaching or practising the doctrine of deposing kings excommunicated for heresy, by any authority whatsoever, as repugnant to the fundamental laws of the nation, as injurious

to

to sovereign power, and as destructive to peace and government.

5. Catholics believe that the *Bishop of Rome*, successor to St, Peter, *is the head of the whole Catholic Church; in which sense this Church may therefore be stiled Roman Catholic*, because an universal body united under one visible head. Nevertheless,

6. It is no matter of faith to believe that the *Pope is in* himself *infallible*, separated from the Church, even in expounding the faith; by consequence, papal definitions or decrees, taken exclusively from a General Council, or universal acceptance of the Church, oblige none, under the pain of heresy, to an interior assent.

7. Nor do Catholics, as Catholics, believe that the Pope has any direct or indirect authority over the temporal power and jurisdiction of Princes. Hence, if the Pope should pretend to absolve or dispense with his Majesty's subjects from their allegiance, on account of heresy or schism, such dispensation would be vain and null, and all Catholic subjects, notwithstanding such dispensation or absolution, would be still bound in conscience to defend their King and country, at the hazard of their lives and fortunes (as far as Protestants would be bound) even against the Pope himself, should he invade the nation.

8. As for the *problematical disputes or errors of particular divines*, in this or any other matter whatsoever, we are in no wise responsible for them; nor are Catholics, as such, justly punishable on their account. But,

9. As for the King killing doctrine, or murder of Princes excommunicated for heresy, it is universally admitted in the Catholic Church, and expressly so declared in the Council of Constance, that such doctrine is impious and execrable, being contrary to the known laws of God and nature.

10. *Personal misdemeanors*, of what nature soever, *ought not to be imputed to the body of Catholics, when not justifiable by the tenets of their faith and doctrine.* For which reason, though the stories of the Irish cruelties, or powder-plot, had been exactly true, (which yet, for the most part, are notoriously mis-related) nevertheless Catholics, as such, ought not to suffer for such offences, any more than the eleven Apostles ought to have suffered for the treachery of Judas.

11. It is a fundamental truth in our religion, that no power on earth can license men to lie, to forswear or perjure themselves, to massacre their neighbours, or destroy their native country, on pretence of promoting the Catholic Cause or Religion. Furthermore, all pardons or dispensations, granted, or pretended to be

be granted, in order to any ſuch ends or deſigns, could have no other validity or effect than to add ſacrilege and blaſphemy to the above mentioned crimes.

12. The doctrine of equivocation, or mental reſervation, however wrongfully imputed to the Catholic religion, was never taught or approved by the Church as any part of her belief: on the contrary, ſimplicity and godly ſincerity are conſtantly inculcated by her as truly Chriſtian virtues, neceſſary to the conſervation of juſtice, truth, and common ſecurity.

SECTION III.

1. Every Catholic believes that when a ſinner repents of his ſins, from the bottom of his heart, and acknowledges his tranſgreſſions to God and his miniſters, the diſpenſers of the myſteries of Chriſt, reſolving to turn from his evil ways, and bring forth fruits worthy of repentance, there is then, and not otherwiſe, an authority left by Chriſt to abſolve ſuch a penitent ſinner from his ſins; which authority Chriſt gave to his Apoſtles and their ſucceſſors, the Biſhops and Prieſts of his Church, in thoſe words, when he ſaid, *Receive ye the Holy Ghoſt, whoſe ſins you ſhall forgive, they are forgiven unto them.*

2. Though no creature whatſoever can make condign ſatisfaction, either for the guilt of ſin or the pain eternal due to it, this ſatisfaction being proper to Chriſt our Saviour only, yet penitent ſinners, redeemed by Chriſt, may, as members of Chriſt, in ſome meaſure ſatisfy by prayer, faſting, alms-deeds, and other works of piety, for temporal pain, which, in the order of Divine Juſtice, ſometimes remains due, after the guilt of ſin and pain eternal have been remitted. Such penitential works are, notwithſtanding, no otherwiſe ſatisfactory, than as joined and applied to that ſatisfaction which Jeſus made upon the Croſs, in virtue of which all our good works find a grateful acceptance in the ſight of God.

3. The guilt of ſin, or pain eternal due to it, is never remitted by what Catholics call Indulgences; but only ſuch temporal puniſhments as remain due after the guilt is remitted: *thoſe indulgences being nothing elſe than a mitigation or relaxation of canonical penances*, enjoined by the paſtors of the Church on penitent ſinners, according to their ſeveral degrees of demerit. And if abuſes and miſtakes have been ſometimes committed, either in point of granting or gaining indulgences through the remiſſneſs or ignorance of particular perſons, contrary to the ancient cuſtom and diſcipline of the Church, ſuch abuſes or miſtakes cannot reaſonably

reaſonably be charged on the Church, or rendered matters of deriſion, in prejudice to her faith and diſcipline.

4. Catholics hold there is a purgatory, that is to ſay, a place or ſtate where ſouls departing this life, with remiſſion of their ſins as to the eternal guilt or pain, but yet obnoxious to ſome temporal puniſhment ſtill remaining due, or not perfectly freed from the blemiſh of ſome defects or deordinations, are purged before their admittance into heaven, where nothing that is defiled can enter.

5. Catholics alſo hold, that ſuch ſouls, ſo detained in purgatory, being the living members of Jeſus Chriſt, are relieved by the prayers and ſuffrages of their fellow-members here on earth: but where this place is, or of what nature or quality the pains are, how long ſouls may be there detained, in what manner the ſuffrages made in their behalf are applied, whether by way of ſatisfaction or interceſſion, &c. are queſtions ſuperfluous, and impertinent, as to faith.

6. No man, though juſt, can merit either an increaſe of ſanctity in this life, or eternal glory in the next, independently on the merits and paſſion of Jeſus Chriſt; but the good works of a juſt man proceeding from grace and charity, are ſo far acceptable to God, as to be, through his goodneſs and ſacred promiſes, truly meritorious of eternal life.

7. It is an article of the Catholic faith, that, in the moſt holy Sacrament of the Euchariſt, there is truly and really contained the body of Chriſt, which was delivered for us, and his blood which was ſhed for the remiſſion of ſins: the ſubſtance of bread and wine being, by the power of Chriſt, changed into the ſubſtance of his bleſſed body and blood, the ſpecies or appearances of bread and wine ſtill remaining—But,

8. Chriſt is not preſent in this ſacrament according to his natural way of exiſtence, that is, with extenſion of parts, &c. but in a ſupernatural manner, one and the ſame in many places, his preſence therefore is real and ſubſtantial, but ſacramental, not expoſed to the external ſenſes, or obnoxious to corporal contingencies.

9. Neither is the body of Chriſt in this holy ſacrament ſeparated from his blood, or his blood from his body, or either of them diſunited from his ſoul and divinity, but all and whole living Jeſus is entirely contained under each ſpecies; ſo that whoſoever receives under one kind is truly partaker of the whole ſacrament, and no wiſe deprived either of the body or blood of Chriſt. True it is,

10. Our Saviour Jeſus Chriſt left unto us his body and blood under two diſtinct ſpecies or kinds; in doing of which, he inſtituted

ſtituted not only a ſacrament, but alſo a ſacrifice, a commemorative ſacrifice diſtinctly ſhewing his death and bloody paſſion until he come; for as the ſacrifice of the Croſs was performed by a diſtinct effuſion of blood, ſo is that ſacrifice commemorated in that of the altar, by a diſtinction of the ſymbols. Jeſus therefore is here given not only to us, but for us, and the Church is thereby enriched with a true, proper, and propitiatory ſacrifice uſually termed the Maſs.

11. *Catholics renounce all divine worſhip and adoration of images or pictures. God alone we worſhip and adore;* nevertheleſs we place pictures in Churches to reduce our wandering thoughts, and enliven our memories towards heavenly things. Further, we allow a certain honour to be ſhewn to the images of Chriſt and his ſaints, beyond what is due to every profane figure; not that we believe any divinity or virtue to reſide in them, for which they ought to be honoured, but becauſe the honour given to pictures is referred to the prototype or thing repreſented. In like manner,

12. There is a kind of honour and reſpect due to the Bible, to the Croſs, to the name of Jeſus, to Churches, to the Sacraments, &c. as things peculiarly appertaining to God, alſo to the glorious Saints in heaven, as the friends of God, and to Kings, Magiſtrates, and Superiors on earth; to whom honour is due, honour may be given, without any derogation to the majeſty of God, or that divine worſhip which is appropriate to him.—Moreover,

13. Catholics believe that the bleſſed Saints in heaven, repleniſhed with charity, pray for us their fellow-members here on earth; that they rejoice at our converſion; that, ſeeing God, they ſee and know him in all things ſuitable to their happy ſtate: but God may be inclined to hear their requeſts made in our behalf, and for their ſakes may grant us many favours; therefore we believe it is good and profitable to deſire their interceſſion; and that this manner of invocation is no more injurious to Chriſt our Mediator, than it is for one Chriſtian to beg the prayers of another in this world. Notwithſtanding which, Catholics are not taught ſo to rely on the prayers of others, as to neglect their own duty to God; in imploring his divine mercy and goodneſs; in mortifying the deeds of the fleſh; in deſpiſing the world; in loving and ſerving God and their neighbour; in following the footſteps of Chriſt our Lord, who is the way, the truth, and the life, to whom be honour and glory for ever and ever. *Amen.*

No. IV.

Copy of the Convention between the French Government and his Holineſs the Pope Pius VII.

Ratified the 23d Fructidor, Year 9, (10th September, 1801).

The Chief Conſul of the French Republic, and his Holineſs the Sovereign Pontiff, Pius the VII. have named as their reſpective plenipotentiaries,

The Chief Conſul, the Citizens Joſeph Bonaparte, Counſellor of State; Cretet, Counſellor of State, and Bernier, Doctor of Divinity, Curate of St. Laud d'Angers; furniſhed with full powers:

His Holineſs, his Eminence Monſeigneur Hercule Conſalvi, Cardinal of the Holy Roman Church, Deacon of St. Agathe *ad Suburram*, his Secretary of State; Joſeph Spina, Archbiſhop of Corinth, Domeſtic Prelate to his Holineſs, Attendant on the Pontifical Throne; and Father Caſelli, his Holineſs's Adviſer on points of Theology; in like manner furniſhed with full powers in due form:

Who, after exchanging their full powers, have concluded the following Convention:

Convention between the French Government and his Holineſs the Pope Pius VII.

The Government of the Republic acknowledges that the Catholic, Apoſtolical, and Roman Religion, is the religion of the great majority of French citizens.

His Holineſs, in like manner, acknowledges that this ſame religion has derived, and is likely to derive, the greateſt benefit and the greateſt ſplendour from the eſtabliſhment of the Catholic worſhip in France, and from its being openly profeſſed by the Conſuls of the Republic.

This mutual acknowledgment being made, in conſequence, as well for the good of religion, as for the maintenance of interior tranquillity, they have agreed as follows:

Article I. The Catholic, Apoſtolical, and Roman religion ſhall be freely exercifed in France. *Its ſervice ſhall be publicly performed, conformably to the regulations of police which the government ſhall judge neceſſary for the public tranquillity.*

II. There ſhall be made by the Holy See, in concert with the government, a new diviſion of French dioceſes.

III. His Holineſs ſhall declare to the titular French Biſhops that he expects from them, with the firmeſt confidence, every ſacrifice for the ſake of peace and unity—even that of their ſees.

After this exhortation, if they ſhould refuſe the ſacrifice commanded for the good of the church, (a refuſal, nevertheleſs, which his Holineſs by no means expects), *the ſees of the new diviſion ſhall be governed by biſhops appointed as follows*:

IV. *Within three months after the publication of his Holineſs's bull, the Chief Conſul ſhall preſent to the archbiſhoprics and biſhoprics of the new diviſion. His Holineſs ſhall confer canonical inſtitution, according to the forms eſtabliſhed for France before the revolution* (avant le changement de government).

V. *The nomination to the biſhoprics which become vacant in future ſhall likewiſe belong to the Chief Conſul*, and canonical inſtitution ſhall be adminiſtered by the Holy See, conformably to the preceding article.

VI. The biſhops, before they enter upon their functions, ſhall take, before the Chief Conſul, the oath of fidelity which was in uſe before the revolution, expreſſed in the following words:

"I ſwear and promiſe to God, upon the Holy Evangeliſts, to preſerve obedience and fidelity to the government eſtabliſhed by the conſtitution of the French Republic. I likewiſe promiſe to carry on no correſpondence, to be preſent at no converſation, to form no connection, whether within the territories of the Republic or without, which may, in any degree, diſturb the public tranquillity: and if, in my dioceſe or elſewhere, I diſcover that any thing is going forward to the prejudice of the ſtate, I will immediately communicate to government all the information I poſſeſs."

VII. Eccleſiaſtics of the ſecond order ſhall take the ſame oath before the civil authorities appointed by the government.

VIII. The following formula of prayer ſhall be recited at the end of divine ſervice in all the Catholic churches of France.

Domine, ſalvam fac Rempublicam,
Domine, ſalvos fac Conſules.

IX. The biſhops ſhall make a new diviſion of the pariſhes in their dioceſes; which, however, ſhall not take effect till after it is ratified by government.

X. The biſhops ſhall have the appointment of the pariſh prieſts.

Their

Their choice ſhall not fall but on perſons approved by government.

XI. The biſhops may have a chapter in their cathedral, and a ſeminary for the dioceſe, without the government being obliged to endow them.

XII. All the metropolitan, cathedral, parochial, and other churches, which have not been alienated, neceſſary to public worſhip, ſhall be placed at the diſpoſal of the biſhops.

XIII. His Holineſs, for the ſake of peace and the happy re-eſtabliſhment of the Catholic religion, declares, that neither he nor his ſucceſſors will diſturb in any manner thoſe who have acquired the alienated property of the church; and that in conſequence, that property, and every part of it, ſhall belong for ever to them, their heirs and aſſigns.

XIV. The government ſhall grant a ſuitable ſalary to biſhops and pariſh prieſts, whoſe dioceſes and pariſhes are compriſed in the new diviſion.

XV. The government ſhall likewiſe take meaſures to enable French Catholics, who are ſo inclined, to diſpoſe of their property for the ſupport of religion.

XVI. His Holineſs recogniſes in the Chief Conſul of the French Republic the ſame rights and prerogatives in religious matters which the ancient government enjoyed.

XVII. It is agreed between the contracting parties, that in caſe any of the ſucceſſors of the preſent Chief Conſul ſhould not be a Roman Catholic, the rights and prerogatives mentioned in the foregoing articles, as well as the nomination to the biſhops' ſees, ſhall be regulated, with regard to him, by a new convention.

The ratification ſhall be exchanged at Paris in the ſpace of forty days.

Done at Paris, the 26th Meſſidor, year 9 of the French Republic.

(Signed) JOSEPH BONAPARTE.
HERCULES, Cardinalis Conſalvi.
JOSEPH, Archiep. Corinthi.
BERNIER.
F. CAROLUS CASELLI.

Note A.

" Some officers of the garrifon urged Lord Lucan and Lord Gallmoy, the commanders of the Irifh army, to break off the treaty, alleging that they could now raife the fiege, which would give fuch fpirits to the Catholics, and fo deprefs the befiegers, that they might yet recover Ireland; and the more fo as they were certain of more aid from France. What was the reply of Lords Lucan and Gallmoy? They faid they confidered themfelves pledged in honour to deliver up Limerick and Ireland to the Proteftants; and they did fo, depending on their faith and truth to preferve inviolate the rights of the Catholics under the articles."——*Mr. Keogh's Speech at the Catholic Meeting, Oct.* 31, 1792.

Note B.

A Letter from Dr. Butler, *Titular Archbifhop of Cafhel, to Lord* Kenmare.

Thurles, December 27, 1786.

My dear and honoured Lord,

I am not a little impatient to impart to your Lordfhip my thoughts on a late publication, entitled, "*The prefent ftate of the Church of Ireland.*" It is written by Dr. Woodward, Bifhop of Cloyne; and, in the fhort fpace of twelve days, has already paffed through four editions. Whoever has feen the Addrefs to the Nobility and Gentry of the Proteftant Church, and reads this Second Pamphlet, cannot but look upon them as *both* defigned to undo all that has been done in favour of Roman Catholics; as they tend to undermine the primary title the Roman Catholics had to the protection of government and the confidence of their fellow-fubjects. The unjuft and falfe ftrictures his Lordfhip makes on the fincerity of the oaths of the Roman

Roman Catholic Biſhops, concur to effect this in the minds of thoſe who can or will be impoſed on by what his Lordſhip ſo confidently aſſerts. For certainly, if the oaths of the Roman Catholic Prelates can no more be depended on, all claim to a legal exiſtence for us in the ſtate ceaſes. We are all deſigning and moſt dangerous enemies: like the viper in the fable, we only ſought the warmth of protection to gnaw the boſom which gave the reviving heat. His Lordſhip, to eſtabliſh and enforce what he advances with regard to our oaths, by ſome new argument which, from not having been uſed before, had never been blunted by the ſhield of truth, brings forth *a letter of a Monſignor Ghilini*, Nuncio at Bruſſels, *written in the year* 1768, from amidſt the duſt of oblivion, where it would otherwiſe have, as it deſerved, remained till doomſday; notwithſtanding the moſt ſtrangely miſapplied *encomiums beſtowed on it by Dr. Bourke:* encomiums, which I know, from the letters the ſaid *Nuncio* wrote to me, before I left the Continent, expreſſive of his own alarmed feelings, after cool reflection, on the impropriety and indiſcretion of ſaid letter, he would have willingly ſpared the Doctor. Nothing, to be ſure, but an *enthuſiaſtic* partiality for *ſcholaſtic opinions*, which Dr. Bourke, perhaps, had formerly, when profeſſor, defended, (as *ſome* Ultromantaniſts have done, to their reproach and the diſcredit of religion, with as much warmth of debate as if thoſe opinions had been acknowledged Articles of Faith, which they were ſupporting againſt unbelievers) can any way extenuate Dr. Bourke's imprudence, to call it by no harſher name, in publiſhing ſuch a letter. The Doctor ſhould have reflected, that the opinions alluded to by the Nuncio, however unnoticed they may be ſuffered to paſs in a country like Italy, where the Sovereign and all the ſubjects are of the Roman Catholic religion, they cannot be conſidered in the ſame light in this kingdom, whereof the King and principal ſubjects are proteſtants, and two thirds, at leaſt, of the inhabitants are of our communion. *Here* ſuch opinions, if maintained, could not but be prejudicial, by alarming the Sovereign, and becoming a conſtant ſource of jealouſy and diſſenſion betwixt fellow-ſubjects.—This, I recal to mind, was what I alleged to Cardinal Mareſuſchi, who was, at the time the oath was propoſed, our Cardinal Protector, (that is, as your Lordſhip knows, the Cardinal entruſted by his Holineſs with the *ſuperintendance* of our eccleſiaſtical affairs in Ireland), as a *reaſon* why the Roman Catholic biſhops thought themſelves called upon to declare, in the public manner they did, that they found nothing in the teſt of allegiance, held out by the legiſlature to the Roman Catholics of Ireland, contrary to the principles of the

the Roman Catholic faith; and, *therefore, that the* opinions *disclaimed by that oath never made part of our creed. The Cardinal, in his answer, expressed the fullest approbation of my sentiments; which approbation* of his Eminence was afterwards *confirmed by the Pope and the Congregation de Propaganda Fide*, approving also of the said test of allegiance: of all which approbations I have *authentic vouchers* by me; the *very* letters written on the occasion to and from the Sacred Congregation. I shewed *these* letters to Lord Pery, when he was Speaker of the House of Commons, at Sir Robert Staples's, and I shewed him again, in Dublin, another letter which I received from the same Congregation, two years after, expressive of their Eminencies' thanks for my diligence in fulfilling what I owed to my station and religion, since the time I came into the kingdom. Now, my dear Lord, I hope I may venture to say, without risking the imputation of vanity or falsehood, that I was most particularly warm and active in promoting the taking of the Test Oath*, after I had publicly approved of it at the head of my Suffragans, in the year 1775; an æra which I always called to mind with new felt pleasure; and consequently, the approbation of my conduct, *during all that time*, was of itself, had I no other proofs of the Congregation's having approved the Test, tantamount to an approbation. Lord Pery, when I shewed him that letter of the Congregation acknowledged it was; so did his Grace the Primate, when I had the honour, on being introduced to him by your Lordship, to mention it to him.

But that nothing might be wanting, in our power, to consign the letter of the Nuncio to eternal oblivion, and that no one of our people might be ever affected by it, We, (I mean the Roman Catholic Prelates of Munster) in a meeting we held at Thurles, soon after the one near Cork, in 1775, passed our *decided censure* upon the Hibernia Dominicana and its Supplement: which censure we, indeed, at first, signified only to our clergy; not thinking it prudent to make known to the people a work of the stamp of the Hibernia Dominicana; which, from its being written in Latin, and bearing a title which was not likely to attract the attention of those who understood that language, would, as I said before, in all probability have remained for ever unknown to them. Our censure was well known at Rome, without being considered there, in the smallest degree, obnoxious to the Holy See. The original, subscribed to by the bishops, I providentially kept by me; not knowing but the time might come, when some one or other would, through ignorance or false zeal, profit of a discovery of the Nuncio's letter, and make use of it as a proper weapon to give what he might think the

* Reg. 13. 14. Geo. 3. c. 3.

the deadly blow to all our fond hopes of protection and confidence from government and our fellow-subjects. My apprehension of such an event, your Lordship sees, by Dr. Woodward's work, was not groundless. At the same time, had I not such a formal and avowed condemnation to produce, the letters from the Sacred Congregation and the Roman Catholic Bishops of the whole kingdom after the most mature deliberation, approving the Test, whereby they solemnly declared, in the face of the whole world, their disbelief and abhorrence of the *opinions* alluded to by the Nuncio, was more than sufficient to obviate the ill-grounded insinuations his Lordship of Cloyne has held forth.

As a public and formal answer will, I hope, be given to his Lordship of Cloyne's Strictures, I'll leave to the writer thereof (that I may not spin out this letter to an unnecessary length) to enlarge more fully on what I here only sketch out. For a public answer must be given. The consciousness of our *inviolable attachment* to our oaths of allegiance; our lively sense of what we owe to our sacred characters; our *sincere* wish to promote and preserve that *long desired* mutual confidence, which had happily begun to warm and link in social union the minds or persons of different persuasions, call on us to repel, in the most earnest and public manner, any attempt to undermine what cannot but be most precious to us.

The author of the public reply to his Lordship's strictures will not fail, I am confident, to paint in the most pathetic manner what our feelings must be, on seeing ourselves traduced as we are to the public; and that by the very Bishop to the neighbourhood of whose diocess I and my Suffragans, the Roman Catholic Prelates of Munster, had speedily repaired, to oppose, *as far as in us lay*, with our united efforts, in the morning of these troubles, the unwarrantable attempts made against ecclesiastical authority. His Lordship may be also more clearly informed by him of the nature of a Nuncio's commission, with regard to the Roman Catholics of this kingdom: his Lordship will find it quite different from what he represents it; and that so far are a Nuncio's sentiments from being looked upon as decisions of the Church, that Roman Catholic Bishops have dissented, and may dissent from the Roman Legate, without apprehension of guilt in all that does not affect the established principles of faith and christian morality. In the letter alluded to, your Lordship cannot but have observed, the Nuncio gives only *his own notions;* which, strange as they appear, can be easily accounted for, in one, who being educated in the Pope's dominions, and being his public Ambassador, may, from *too warm*

warm a desire of aggrandizing the temporal power of his Sovereign, extend too far the prerogatives of his spiritual jurisdiction.

As to the oath taken by the Roman Catholic Bishops at their consecration, and printed in the Roman Pontifical, which Dr. Woodward brings forth as an *auxiliary* proof how little our oaths of allegiance are to be depended on, I shall just observe, that his Lordship has entirely misconceived both the intention and words of the oath. A little reflection would have made his Lordship sensible, that said oath is *by no means inconsistent* with the subject's allegiance to his *Prince;* that Sovereigns as jealous and tenacious of their rights as Sovereigns can be, permit said oath to be taken by the Roman Catholic Bishops in their dominions: which they evidently never would consent to, but would, on the contrary, strenuously oppose, if they could think it infringed in the least on their rights, or paved the way to *papal encroachments.* It is well known *this very oath*, of which Dr. Woodward speaks, is taken by all the Bishops consecrated in France, Germany, Spain, and in all the different kingdoms and republics on the continent—The Bishops of the republic of Venice *all* take it. Fra. Paoli himself, in his warm Defence of the Rights of the Venetian Republic against the claims of the Court of Rome, (a work Dr. Woodward cannot be a stranger to), never points out to that jealous Senate the oaths taken by Roman Catholic Bishops at their consecration, as affording a ground to suspect their fealty to the state. This oath was even taken in Holland, under the eyes of the States themselves, by the Pope's Vicar Apostolic for that country, who must generally be a Bishop, and consequently conform to the Rubrics of the Pontifical, which he does without becoming obnoxious to the Dutch. The King of Prussia apprehends no danger from it to his dominions, though he knows full well the Bishops of Silesia, of whose loyal sentiments he is more particularly interested in being secure, take also said oath at their consecration. Nay, the King of Great Britain, our most gracious Sovereign, whom may the Almighty long preserve, is no way alarmed at having a Roman Catholic Bishop in Canada; being *fully* assured that a Roman Catholic Bishop in Canada will be as earnest to oppose all papal encroachments as his confreres in England were in opposing, (according even to his Lordship of Cloyne's acknowledgment, p. 48.) in the earlier days of the British empire, those of the Sovereign Pontiffs. For every discerning person cannot but know, on the least reflection, that none of us, to make use of the *very* words of the great *Bossuet, Bishop of Meaux*, ever engage ourselves by this

this oath to any thing that is contrary to our conſcience, or the ſervice of our King and country: far from thinking we prejudice *any* of theſe, it is even expreſſed in the oath, that we take it without prejudice to our ſtate, *ſalvo meo ordine*. The ſubmiſſion which is ſworn to the Pope in ſpirituals, is of a different order from what we naturally owe our Prince in temporals, and without proteſting, we have always well underſtood, that one does not interfere with the other.—So far that learned and judicious Prelate.

Your Lordſhip will find theſe very words of Boſſuet, in the beginning of the firſt chapter of the 7th book of the Variations: —they clearly account for ſaid oath's being ſo univerſally taken by all the Roman Catholic Biſhops in both Catholic and Proteſtant ſtates. The SALVO MEO ORDINE removes all fear of the oath's injuring the allegiance due to other Princes. The oath itſelf, at the beginning, was only taken by the Biſhops of the Pope's eccleſiaſtical territories, who from being ſubjects of the Pope, as a temporal Sovereign, ſwear fealty to him both in ſpirituals and temporals, which is not the caſe with Biſhops, who do not belong to the Pope's dominions; and hence, when a deſire of conformity with the Biſhops that are immediately ſubject to the Pope, made it, by degrees, cuſtomary for the Roman Catholic Biſhops throughout the whole world to take the ſaid oath at their conſecration, they all took care to profeſs *plainly and publicly*, by the clauſe SALVO MEO ORDINE, that they did not bind themſelves down to any thing in ſaid oath, but in as far as it was compatible with the ſituation of every Biſhop under their reſpective Sovereigns, and the duty he eſſentially owes to them. The oath is almoſt of 800 years date; time, ſurely, ſufficient for every Sovereign to know the meaning of it.

The words of the oath, *Hereticos perſequar et impugnabo*, which his Lordſhip of Cloyne repreſents as *ſo alarming* to the Proteſtant intereſt, far from meaning what his Lordſhip ſeems to think, imply nothing more than the obligation every Biſhop takes upon himſelf, to be ever earneſt in oppoſing and refuting, by the ſpiritual weapons of the goſpel, all broachers of doctrines contrary to its principles.

Theſe, my dear Lord, are the thoughts which occurred to me on reading that part of Dr. Woodward's work, which attacks the conſcientious ſincerity of Roman Catholic Biſhops. Thoughts, which I was moſt anxious to communicate to a Nobleman of my own religion, whoſe zealous and ſucceſsful exertions in ſuppreſſing the diſturbances in the county of Kerry, have met with the deſerved applauſe of government and of the

Clergy of both communions. On that account, I look up to your Lordſhip as the beſt entitled to avail yourſelf, with every advantage, of the facts I have mentioned, in order to prevent or efface the very unfavourable impreſſions Dr. Woodward's ſtrictures on us may make, or have made, on the public, by miſrepreſenting the Nuncio's letter as a deciſion of our Church, and the oath Biſhops take at their conſecration, as incompatible with our allegiance.

I have the honour to be,

With the ſincereſt attachment and eſteem,

My Dear Lord,

Your Lordſhip's moſt obedient Servant,

And affectionate Kinſman,

JAMES BUTLER.

Note C.

Beſides the various inſtances which have been ſtated of the diſpoſition of the Proteſtants in various parts of Ireland to act with liberality towards the Catholics, the following have occurred within the laſt twelve months —Reſolutions have been publiſhed by the Grand Juries of the counties of Kilkenny and Galway in favour of emancipation.—The Proteſtant inhabitants of Newry, at a public meeting convened by the Seneſchal, agreed to a declaration expreſſing their wiſh to have every thing conceded to them, provided they would conſent to permit the King to nominate their Biſhops.—The principal Nobility and Gentry of the counties of Tipperary, Meath, and Waterford, have publiſhed declarations of their ſentiments in favour of emancipation.—At general meetings of the Freeholders of the counties of Galway, Roſcommon, and Sligo, unanimous reſolutions have been agreed to, approving of that meaſure.—Thirty Orange Lodges in the North of Ireland publiſhed an expoſition of their principles laſt July, wherein they ſtated that the object of their inſtitution was to reſiſt republicaniſm, and not religious conſiderations.—They likewiſe declared their intention not again to celebrate the Battle of the Boyne.

www.ingramcontent.com/pod-product-compliance
Lightning Source LLC
Chambersburg PA
CBHW030301100426
42812CB00002B/521
* 9 7 8 1 5 8 4 7 7 3 1 0 8 *